Don't Cheat the Butterfly is God's secret weapon! I found myself holding my breath as I turned the page. The strategies contained in this book are applicable to so many areas and seasons of our lives, not just the ones Kristen has so transparently and courageously written about. The contents will not only inform you, but empower you to come through victorious. I have already added the strategies Kristen Smeltzer presents to my spiritual arsenal. I recommend that everyone read this book. I will definitely pass it on!

Chris Anthony-Lansdowne
Host of *Adventures in Odyssey*, Focus on the Family

An amazing work that will have an endless effect, this testimony of God's love and faithfulness during times of trial and darkness will change lives. Kristen Smeltzer instills fresh hope in the God who delivers His people out of the darkness and into His marvelous light, and who is continually preparing a future for us beyond what we could ask or think.

Cal Pierce
Director, Healing Rooms Ministries

Don't Cheat the Butterfly is a testimony of hope, so badly needed by so many. As a generation, many are offended with God. We also seem to be under constant attack with thoughts of worthlessness, hopelessness and failures galore. This keeps us from rising up into our true identity in Christ. We all need to hear Kristen's testimony of how to walk through our offenses with God and overcome such an attack on our identity.

I encourage all to let the warfare for Zachary David warn and inform you. Buy the book, put it to work—and give it away.

John Loren Sandford
Co-Founder of Elijah House, Inc.
and Best-Selling Author of *Transformation of the Inner Man*

For anyone who knows there are forces in this world beyond our sight, anyone fighting for the hearts and souls of their children, anyone who needs hope when there is none to grasp, this is a must-read book. With raw vulnerability and penetrating spiritual insight, Kristen Smeltzer tells a true story of her son that will go deep into your heart, soul, and spirit.

James L. Rubart
Bestselling Author of *The Long Journey to Jake Palmer*
2017 Carol Award Winner, Speculative
Christy Award Winner

I too have been one who has sat in front of "Zachary," staring into his eyes, trying my best to offer a glimpse of hope. This man was my husband, who in his mind, felt like he was never going to get free from the pain and torment. The good news is that our God is so good and He only wants the best for each of His kids. Kristen Smeltzer tells it like it is. There is power in the process and through it all, she has written a very heartfelt, helpful book that will not only strengthen you but give you tools to reach out and help others.

Kathy Vallotton
Senior Leadership Team – Bethel Church, Redding, CA and
Co-Founder of Bethel School of Supernatural Ministry

We believe that God has given Kristen a timely depth of insight into a spiritual struggle that is so deceptive that the number of those taken captive by it seems to be exponential and spreading like wildfire by the day. Each one of us, I'm sure, has been affected in some way, either by our own experience with "identity theft" or by that of a loved one. With Kristen's story comes understanding and direction to help us through the process and fight for the victory that Jesus died for us to have. With that said, no matter where you are at in your walk with God, this is a *must read* for every believer, because it is crucial that the very foundation of our life should be knowing who God is and who He says we are.

Stuart and Sharon Young
YWAM Honolulu Director of Training, 1984-1992

Kristen Smeltzer has been a friend for thirty years. She's a healthy, loving, joyful Christian who did well at raising her boys. She didn't expect to find herself in a battle for one son's destiny, but then, millions of parents have found themselves facing the same battle. Spiritual forces are hard at work in our culture to misidentify both God and our children. Kristen's gripping story confronts us with the spiritual nature of the battle we face, while giving us practical, biblical strategies that work. It's a hopeful, encouraging story and a must read for parents.

Bill Dwyer
Senior Pastor, The Valley Vineyard, Reseda, CA

Don't Cheat the Butterfly: A Battle, a Strategy, and a Mind Transformed
Copyright © 2025, Kristen Smeltzer

All rights reserved. No part of this manuscript may be used or reproduced in any matter whatsoever without written permission from the publisher, except in the case of brief quotations embodied in critical articles and reviews.
For more information or bulk orders, please contact info@destinyoak.com.

Second Edition: Revised and Expanded
Previously Published as *Who Do You Say I Am?*,
by Kristen M. Smeltzer, ©2017.
(Paperback ISBN #9780999562888)

Unless otherwise identified, Scripture quotations are taken from the New King James Version. Copyright © 1982 by Thomas Nelson, Inc. Used by permission. All rights reserved. Scripture quotations marked (AMP) are taken from the Amplified ® Bible, Copyright © 2015 by The Lockman Foundation. Used by permission. Scripture quotations marked (NIV) are taken from the HOLY BIBLE, NEW INTERNATIONAL VERSION, Copyright © 1973, 1978, 1984, 2011 International Bible Society. Used by permission of Zondervan. All rights reserved. Scripture quotations marked (ESV) are taken from the ESV ® Bible (The Holy Bible, English Standard Version ®), copyright 2001 by Crossway, a publishing ministry of Good News Publishers. Used by permission. All rights reserved.

PLEASE NOTE: All emphasis within Scripture quotations is the author's own. The publisher chooses to capitalize pronouns that refer to the Father, Son and Holy Spirit, while not acknowledging satan by capitalizing his name unless beginning a sentence.

Library of Congress Cataloging-in-Publication Data

Names: Smeltzer, Kristen, 1963- author.
Title: Don't cheat the butterfly : a battle, a strategy, and a mind transformed / Kristen Smeltzer
Description: 2nd Edition: Revised and Expanded •Destiny Oak, 2025
Library of Congress Control Number: 2024919027
Identifiers: ISBN 9780999562833 (paperback) •ISBN 9780999562857 (eBook) •ISBN 9780999562895 (Kindle) •ISBN 9780999562840 (Audiobook)
Subjects: BISAC: RELIGION—Christian Living—Spiritual Growth. RELIGION—Christian Living—Spiritual Warfare. RELIGION—Christian Living—Inspirational.
LC Record available at: https://lccn.loc.gov/2024919027

DESTINY
OAK

Cover Design: Stephen Vosloo at StephenVosloo.com | Images Courtesy of Unsplash
Interior Design: Glenn Bontrager at Fiverr.com/sarco2000

For Worldwide Distribution, Printed in the United States
Hayden, Idaho

DEDICATION

To my God, The Great I AM—Where else would I go? Only You have the words of life. I will sing Your praises for eternity. May I always be "one who touches Your heart."

To my son, Zachary David—How you walked through the Valley of the Shadow of Death moves me still. Your courage, steadfastness and faith have moved mountains. I could not be more proud of the man you have become.

To my husband, Richard—Thank you for being a strength, voice of wisdom and reassurance of God's goodness. I would not wish to go through this life with anyone else by my side.

My sons, Andrew and Jacob—The faith, love and courage I have witnessed through your journeys is no less extraordinary. I am beyond proud to call you sons.

My Grandchildren, Present and Future—Whether already on this earth or not for years to come, you are in my heart. It is my hope you will one day read this account. It's your spiritual heritage. May this testimony give you strength and courage for *your* story, though not yet written. Know I love you and will be cheering you on, long after I leave this earth.

ACKNOWLEDGMENTS

Our Friends and Faithful Prayer Warriors—You stood by us, counseled us and diligently prayed to hold the enemy at bay. A war is never fought single-handedly, and this one was no different. This book is not only a testimony of our extravagant God, but of the courageous warriors who dressed for battle. You know who you are, and I will never forget your part in this victory.

My Parents and Step-Parents—Thank you for supporting me, believing in me and giving me wings to fly. I love you!

My "Daughter-in-Love," Savannah—Zachary chose well. I didn't lose a son. I gained a daughter. Thank you for all your help. Your gifts and talents are only outshone by your beauty within.

Barb, Adele and Genie—The first to read this book and give me incredible advice, help and support. Thank you for your loving sacrifice.

Andrea—Thank you for the title! When you first heard God speak this to you, it helped me walk through my darkest season. It is only fitting that it's now the title of this book. I so appreciate your love and generosity.

CONTENTS

Foreword by Bill Johnson xiii
Preface xv

PART ONE – THE DIVINE BATTLE 1

    Chapter One   The Hunted 3
    Chapter Two   A God-Breathed Battle Plan 13
    Chapter Three   Stepping Through Offense 29
    Chapter Four   It's All In A Name 51
    Chapter Five   Identity Quest 69
    Chapter Six   Don't Cheat the Butterfly 89

PART TWO – SPOILS OF WAR 107

    Chapter Seven   Tilted Scales 109
    Chapter Eight   The Hunted Becomes the Hunter 127
    Chapter Nine   Taking Flight 141

Afterword by Zachary Smeltzer 151

BONUS SECTION – THE ULTIMATE QUESTION 159

The Ultimate Question: A Devotional 161
Lord, I Want To KNOW You 167
Conversational Prayer Guide 169
Journaling Prompts 175
Who Do You Say I AM?: God's Names, Nature and Character 179
Who Do YOU Say I Am?: Who I Am in Christ 193
About the Author 199

FOREWORD

By BILL JOHNSON
Senior Leader of Bethel Church, Redding, CA
Author of *Strengthen Yourself in the Lord* and *God is Good*

I love stories. Jesus often taught in parables because stories are the easiest way to learn a truth. Books with true stories are extra special, because they are usually written after the trauma has run its course, ending with a lesson learned or a redemptive conclusion. Perhaps it's because looking back always adds a perspective that is hard to find in the middle of the experience. This book contains such perspective and so much more.

Don't Cheat the Butterfly is a story of a very rough journey, first in dealing with the thief (identity theft) and then into a profound discovery of our identity in Christ. The victory recorded is beautiful, insightful, and empowering.

We've learned that real faith does not deny the existence of a problem; it just denies the problem a place of influence. Everything God does is to build in us an awareness of identity and purpose so that we can effectively use His name and His authority to see the dreams of heaven accomplished on the earth. The enemy would love nothing more than for us to be distracted from that privilege by the difficulties of life.

Learning to anchor our affections in His Word and presence keeps us living from heaven's perspective. It's the place where we learn the truth of who we are as sons and daughters of a loving Father, commissioned with authority over the enemy.

Many of us have promises from God that we are contending for. And sometimes, for whatever reason, things don't always turn out the way we expect. We cannot allow our experience, or lack of experience, to redefine who God is. It's easy in those moments to want to question God, but we must be careful never to accuse Him. He is not the problem.

The pain and the questions are very real, no doubt. But in those moments, I will bring my pain before Him honestly and say something like, "God, it *feels* like you've betrayed me. But I know that is impossible. It's impossible for you to lie. I know that you are perfectly faithful." In that place, I begin to move out of the bondage of a lie into the liberty of truth.

In *Don't Cheat the Butterfly*, author Kristen Smeltzer beautifully unpacks her family's journey of doing just that. Found on these pages is a road map that will absolutely benefit every reader by leading us into a place of greater strength in the Lord—a place of being totally convinced of the goodness of God.

Revelation 19:10 tells us that "the revelation of Jesus is the spirit of prophecy." In other words, what God has done in another, He is ready and willing to do again in your life. Read this book with expectancy.

PREFACE

But what about you? Who do you say I am?

~Jesus, Matthew 16:15, NIV

THIS STORY REALLY starts with a question: *"Who do you say I am?"* It was a question God had been asking me for quite some time. Years, honestly. I don't know if this is unusual, but He talks to me like that—dropping questions and thought-provoking statements into my mind when I least expect it. These usually send me on a quest of some sort. I initially thought this one was no different, but it definitely was. I didn't understand it at the time, but God was throwing me a lifeline.

When considering His question, in 2009, I thought there was an easy answer. Not easy from the standpoint that any human can ever adequately describe the fullness of God, but easy meaning—that by this time in my 30 years of walking with Him—I thought I knew Him. I thought my heart believed everything my mouth would utter.

The result of my ponderings was an article called "Great Expectations" that I had published in November of that year. It was a prayer, so to speak: a declaration of my faith. I was facing off my current circumstances with the best tool in my toolbox: trusting my God to be all I knew Him to be.

God's question popped up again two years later, in 2011. To say I was going through a serious rough patch was an understatement. I was facing one major trial after another, in every area of my life. My head would pop up out of the water only to be shoved back under, after barely a gasp of air. And I was exhausted.

What I didn't know was that soon I would confront my blackest night. A night containing such fear and sorrow that it would be months before I would have eyes to see God's hand at work. And if I had thought I'd suffered before, this would take it to a whole new level.

Because it's one thing to walk through the depths of hell yourself. It's quite another to have a front row seat for your son's trip there.

PART ONE

The Divine Battle

For the weapons of our warfare are not carnal but mighty in God for pulling down strongholds.

~Apostle Paul, 2 Corinthians 10:4

CHAPTER ONE

The Hunted

This is what the LORD says to you: "Do not be afraid or discouraged because of this vast army. For the battle is not yours, but God's."

-Jahaziel, 2 Chronicles 20:15, NIV

HAVE YOU EVER experienced something in your life you never thought would touch you or your family? Have you ever felt like, "God! I thought we were friends, you and me. I thought you loved me. Why would you allow me to go through this? Why would you allow someone I love to go through this? You don't even seem to be acting according to Your Word!" I have.

It all started on August 3, 2011. It was the summer before our identical twins' senior year of high school and the day before my birthday. Our oldest son, Andrew, had recently moved out and was living on his own. My husband, Richard, and I were asleep in bed, as was Zachary's twin brother, Jacob. Zachary was supposed to be staying the night with a friend. Instead, he came into our room at 2:00 a.m. and shook us awake. He stood over us trembling, and I knew something was terribly wrong.

Zachary appeared desperate. He had a look of terror in his eyes, and I could tell he was not himself. He insisted demons were there and were going to kill him. He implored us to pray for him. And right now!

First, you have to know my son. Even as a kid, he had always been level-headed and wasn't ruled by his emotions. He was mature for his age, honoring and respectful to adults and children alike. He was a leader everywhere he went. He was chosen by his high school as a mentor to incoming freshman. He was co-captain of the basketball team and an "A" student. He was courageous and seemingly unafraid. He wasn't prone to going along with the crowd. And instead of using his popularity to be cruel, he used it to show kindness to others.

For instance, there were occasions when Zachary would befriend insecure students who had trouble fitting in. Rather than keeping his distance, like high school kids often do, Zachary would take them under his wing. He'd invite them over or hang out with them at school, and he would encourage them to believe in themselves. Zachary was not perfect, but he was as near perfect as a son could be. So when the night began to unfold, we could hardly believe it.

Richard and I jumped out of bed and took him into the living room. We prayed and prayed, while Zach continued to grow more distraught, clutching my hand in his. I knew my authority in Christ, as did Richard. We were exercising it to the best of our ability, but whatever was afflicting Zachary was refusing to budge. We realized pretty quickly he was high, and we were shocked.

After an exhausting hour of warring in prayer and still nothing shifting, God gently nudged me to invite Zach to repent to be set free from whatever door he had opened. He immediately began praying. It became evident he was repenting, not only to the Lord, but to us as well. Zachary had always been upright and honest with us and was so sorry he had broken our trust. He confessed he had been doing some things that were out of character for him. We were stunned to find out that over the summer he had started smoking pot with his friends.

Right in front of us, Zachary began to recommit his life to Jesus and petitioned God to rescue him. He soon began to cry, saying God had touched him, he was "back" and the demons were gone. I looked in his eyes and they had indeed returned to normal. My 6'2" son, who was always the tough guy, fell across Richard's lap and began to weep, repeatedly thanking God for setting him free.

After several minutes, Zach sat up, looked us in the eyes and said he felt God just called him into ministry. (Before that night, he had plans to go to college for a degree in business.) I remember thinking as we headed back to our beds, "Wow! This is amazing! We had a one-night blip in the road, and now our son is being called into the ministry! How great is that? All is well." I couldn't have been more wrong.

A CALL TO WAR

What we thought was a beautiful ending to a traumatic night was actually a peaceful beginning, by comparison—the calm before the storm. Starting the next morning, the hounds of hell seemed to have returned in full force, as did the fear and emptiness in Zachary's eyes. It was as if the victory we experienced never occurred and we were reliving the previous night all over again.

Richard and I put our combat boots back on. We rebuked the enemy and what he was trying to do and prayed peace over our son. It seemed to break again. Now that Zachary wasn't high, we thought we could rationalize the experience and explain what had happened. The pot he had smoked had caused a bad trip, and the effects of it would continue to wear off. I encouraged him to drink a lot of water and eat healthy food to flush his system. And once again, I thought this was behind us.

After day three, we realized that whatever had happened to our son was not over. Fear and terror were becoming the norm for Zachary. As one day turned into another, terror permeated more and more hours of his day, as if the initial hours of that dreadful night were stuck on repeat.

More began to surface about what had taken place over the past couple of months. Zachary confessed that at one point earlier that summer, he had lost consciousness while high. During that experience, he said he had died and come out of his body. He watched his friends try to revive him while he watched from above himself. He then believes he went to hell—experiencing demons and terror.

When we first heard this, we thought the pot Zach smoked had to have been laced with something. But on all occasions, Zach smoked off a common joint he and his friends shared, and no one else had a similar reaction.

While in hell, satan told Zachary he was no longer worthy of God's grace and mercy, and was therefore unforgivable and doomed to spend eternity with him. Zachary was told he would be "sent back to earth," but he would no longer be himself. Satan told him another lie that was so vile, it doesn't warrant repeating. Suffice it to say, satan tried to assert a new identity into Zachary, one that shook him to his core. Whether all this really happened or was a hallucination, we don't know. Regardless, it was very real to Zach.

In the midst of that initial terrifying *trip*, Zach called out to Jesus and returned to his body. Unfortunately, as frightening as this experience was, it didn't stop him from smoking pot again later that summer, which consequently led to the pivotal night of August 3rd.

It soon became obvious the battle for Zachary's restoration and healing was in no way complete. We continued to fight for him with everything in us. What we couldn't have known was how long this would last or that we were about to enter the fight of our lives.

STANDARD WEAPONS OF WARFARE

From the beginning of this journey, I knew I was waging a war for my son with the enemy of our souls, and my own intellect would be no match. There were a few tools I had learned in my years of walking with the Lord, and I utilized them. The first of these is to look at your life for any open doors. When we sin, we give the enemy a landing pad. It is as if we are saying, "Come on in and make yourself at home." Continuous willful sin is the easiest way to allow darkness complete access to your life.

When Zachary came into our room on August 3rd and was in obvious torment that wouldn't leave at the name of Jesus, I knew he had given access in some way through sin. In such cases, the best way to close a demonic door is through repentance and forgiveness, and Zachary had done just that. He confessed the things he had been doing over the summer that allowed the enemy to have a proverbial heyday. He not only asked God's forgiveness, but he made a wholehearted choice to completely change his behavior from that point on. Of course he needed God's help and strength, but this was the true desire of his heart. And he had every intention of following through. I knew this was a mark of true repentance—a complete 180-degree turn.

From that dreaded night forward, Zachary immediately began to turn his whole life around. He pulled away from tempting and toxic relationships, and he got rid of anything connected to his former sin and behavior.

We had raised our three sons to love and read the Word of God, and to stand on God's promises for anything life throws at you. And *life* was throwing Zachary quite a curve ball. All on his own, Zachary began to immerse himself in his Bible every day. He put scriptures on the mirror in his bathroom and would read them aloud when he was getting ready in the morning. He dove into the Psalms and read each one as if he was reading about his own life. God's Word is life and healing, and Zachary needed both desperately.

He also started listening to worship music. There was not a time it wasn't playing in his room, even when he left it. Worship and God's Word became needed transfusions of peace, allowing momentary reprieves from the darkness.

Our home became Zachary's haven of safety, and he chose to not leave the house without us. This was his decision, not something we imposed on him. But Zachary was a brave young man, and shrinking back out of fear was not who he was.

We continued to pray and seek God for what He would have us do, so everything could simply return to normal. I was watching Zachary pursue the Lord with everything in him, and I mean everything. It touched my heart, as his mother. I knew it had to be touching the Lord's. Surely this, whatever *this* was, would come to an end shortly.

SHIFTING GEARS

Because Zachary's repentance was sincere, I knew the enemy didn't have a legal right to be there anymore, yet day after long day it continued. And though Zachary was doing all the right things from the sincerity of his heart, he was getting progressively worse. For me, a girl who has always tried "to figure God out" (yes, I understand this is ridiculous), it was making no logical sense.

We continued to do everything we knew to do for Zachary over the next several days. We prayed and fasted together as a family. We cast out and rebuked the enemy. We memorized scripture and stood on the Word of God whenever Zachary was attacked. We sought counsel, prayer and even deliverance ministry. Nothing showed immediate fruit. To our horror, this demon—whatever it was—still seemed to have a foothold.

I want to interject something here. I was not at the time, nor am I still, one to talk about demons. Not that I don't believe they exist. That would be foolish. But I simply don't look for a demon under every rock, or attribute every bad circumstance in my life to a demon. Much of what we go through in life is a result of our own sin and choices, or the result of living in a fallen world. But this was different. This was an assault like nothing I had ever seen or heard of in the past. To put it in Zachary's words today, "Mom, no words could ever express how horrific this was. No one, besides you, will ever really know the depths of what we went through."

But that is true for everyone who walks through darkness. To a large degree, you walk it alone. And while words can provide a blurry snapshot, they can never paint a full portrait.

As Zachary's mom, that snapshot was torturous to watch. Going out in public became a terrifying venture, as Zachary started to see demons everywhere he went. He would see them over people and would know what sins a person was committing based on the demon he saw, and it petrified him. He started hearing voices that spoke more lies to him that brought confusion and fear. We knew it appeared Zach was experiencing a drug-induced schizophrenia.

There were times I would completely melt down. I was not only physically, emotionally and spiritually exhausted…I was terrified. Was this my son's lot now? Was this something we had to *learn to live with*?

Something we would have to *learn to survive*? Was I doing something wrong as his mother? This battle against the spirit of fear was not just Zach's alone. It pounded at the door of my heart continually, threatening to beat the door down.

I wanted desperately to help my son and earnestly desired the best plan of action. Should I take him to a hospital? Seek outside help? It seemed God wasn't coming through fast enough, and I fought for my faith in His goodness and power.

My friends can attest that it wasn't always pretty. I would like to say I was a pillar of strength and faith from the beginning, but that would be a lie. Oh, there were many times when I stood strong and courageous. In fact, in my heart of hearts, my spirit always believed in the greatness of my God. But there were many times when the weakness of my flesh—of my soul—got the best of me, and I struggled for my spirit to prevail.

After receiving some loving prayer and a kind reminder of the miraculous God I serve from some incredible friends, Richard and I went before the Lord for wisdom. We felt God's strong reassurance of what we had felt in our hearts from the start. This was not a mental, chemical or emotional issue for Zachary. This was spiritual.

Please Be Aware: This book is neither about mental illness nor about marijuana. It's about a strategy God gave me to confront *many* trials we face—especially with regard to our identity. I'm *NOT* suggesting that you shouldn't take someone to the doctor if they are exhibiting mental illness. *NOR* am I saying you shouldn't use medicine. *Our* journey is not necessarily a model for *yours*, and you need to hear from the Lord for yourself. However, I feel what is sometimes diagnosed as schizophrenia is actually a demonic attack. And *for us*, this is exactly what we felt God was saying.

We knew beyond a shadow of a doubt Zachary was in a spiritual battle. Therefore, we were to fight this one with spiritual weapons, not ones of flesh and blood. Yes, the dependable weapons of our past warfare didn't seem to be driving back our enemy. But our answers would not come from the wisdom of man. Our help would come from God alone. Again, I cried out desperately for Him to come quickly.

CHAPTER TWO

A God-Breathed Battle Plan

The art of war is simple enough. Find out where your enemy is. Get at him as soon as you can. Strike at him as hard as you can, and keep moving on.

~Ulysses S. Grant

WHEN YOU COME to the end of yourself, you realize God is your only hope. And I was coming to the end of myself rather quickly. Zachary was not only failing to improve, he was becoming a shadow of his former self. I barely recognized him. Zachary came out of the womb sure and strong. Now each day he took hour-long showers, often more than one, to try to escape the madness. He cranked up worship music in the bathroom, not only for the purpose of enveloping himself in peace, but also to drown out his quiet sobs. But I heard. And my heart was breaking and trembling within me.

At this point, I knew I needed a God-breathed war strategy and went before the Lord to ask for one. God was faithful with an immediate response. It didn't seem too profound at the time, but rather simple. I was to teach Zachary, afresh:

1. Who God is: His nature, His names, His attributes, and His character.
2. Who he was: Who Zach was in Christ, and who he was as an individual—his own unique design.

This sent me on a quest. I began to look for scriptures that answered the question, "Who is God?" I also looked for scriptures and promises of who we are in Christ. I wrote many out on little cards and put them in a jar by Zach's bed so they were easily accessible. I even found a CD where the names of God are spoken on a continuous loop, called "I AM: 365 Names of God," by John Paul Jackson. We played this in Zach's room and in our living room repeatedly.

I knew God didn't care so much about Zachary being able to quote scriptures or spout off facts about who He is. God is always after an intimate relationship with us, not how much we know. But the enemy was shouting lies about who Zachary was—and lies about God—into Zach's ears, and they were haunting him. In fact, this wasn't a day-by-day battle anymore. It was becoming minute-by-minute. Zachary lived in constant terror of dying again and returning to the hell he had escaped.

I understood God's strategy would be a launching point to train Zachary to listen to the voice of truth—the Holy Spirit—over the voice of these demons. God's Word would become a firm foundation of truth, upon which a fresh relationship with God could be built.

It didn't take long for me to realize this journey was for me as much as it was for Zachary. God was getting to something much deeper than I even realized. He was going after what our hearts believed of Him. He was going after our expectations.

Two years previous, in 2009, I had written an article called "Great Expectations" for a local Christian publication. In the article I posed the question, "Who *is* God?" I explained that, in response, most would quote scriptures and basic tenets of faith found in the Bible. They would say He is Omnipresent, Omniscient, all-loving, etc. I went on to explain that our theology of God doesn't determine who we believe God to be. Not really. Instead, our daily expectations of His movement in our lives reveal our true beliefs.

I shared that, "in our heart of hearts, who we anticipate God to be—in us and for us—is the true picture of what we believe of God and His character. We may say God is 'this' or 'that.' We might profess He is a God of love and mercy. Yet if we don't expect Him to be loving and merciful *to us*—in tangible ways—we don't truly believe this.

For example, we may *say* things like, 'God works all things together for good.' But if we are not waiting with expectation for our ashes to turn to beauty, this remains head knowledge—not a reflection of our faith in a God who works the impossible on our behalf, simply because He loves us.

One reason for our unbelief is our lack of personal experience, or our disappointments when God doesn't *perform* as we had hoped or believed He should. Yet we can't dismiss the truth of God's Word because we haven't known it to be true in our lives or in a particular situation. Our faith must be founded on what His Word actually says. If God said it, it must be true...period. If it has not been our experience, we must contend for it to be. There can be no other response."

In the article, I explained that holding an expectation of God actually honors Him. A heart of faith-filled expectation says, "I know You are good. I know You are all-powerful. I know You are a loving Father and a faithful friend, and I anticipate You being just that."

At the time of the article's printing, I believed it was written from my past experience. In reality, the article was a picture of what was to come. Its message was definitely a part of me at the time, and came from a deep place in my soul. But beginning in 2011, my expectations of God would go through the fire. God would begin to sear my own message into the depths of my spirit. Unfortunately, at this point, all I could do was smell my burning flesh.

WATCH YOUR MOUTH

In spite of all the repentance, rebuking evil, standing on God's Word, and our acts of faith, the battle did not diminish. Zach would come to me daily with terror in his eyes, often unable to even speak. He'd simply walk up to me and grab my hand, his eyes pleading to make it stop.

In the midst of this, God led me to a unique way to implement the strategy He had given; regarding teaching Zachary afresh who God is and who Zach was. I would tell Zachary to look in my eyes, then I'd look back into his eyes and say, "Who is God?" I would then begin to verbally express the truth of the nature of God: i.e. *His goodness, His greatness, His power and His love.*

I would then ask him, "Who are you?" I always began by telling Zachary his given name, and then I would tell him his identity in Christ—truths found in the Bible. I would also tell him who I believed he was as a person, his own unique design.

For a while, all Zachary could do was listen and nod. The very first time he was able to verbally respond to me, it was more a plea than an answer. I had asked him who God is and all he could say was, "Tell me, Mom." I reiterated, as I had done daily, the nature and names of God. The heartbreak came when I asked him who *he* was. He replied with deep sadness, "I don't know anymore, Mom," to which I replied, "You are Zachary David Smeltzer." I had him repeat his name, out loud. I then spoke scriptures and truths of Zachary's identity in Christ to counteract the enemy's lies, and had him repeat each one. Zachary had these attacks every day, and we did this each time. I knew there was power in him voicing the truths from his own mouth.

Still, I would watch as a war was waged right in front of me between the enemy's lies and God's truth. I could see it on Zach's face. I could see him fighting for truth in his own head and his own heart. On one such occasion, I asked "Who are you?" I could see Zachary doubting his very existence. I knew the enemy was constantly speaking into his ear that he was *no more*. I looked my son intently in the eye and said, "You are Zachary David Smeltzer. Say it."

I still remember his response that day. He said, "Mom! Your mouth is disappearing!" I responded, "Then look in my eyes!" and continued speaking the truth of who he was. Later he explained that my mouth became a black hole and seemed to physically disappear as I spoke these truths. The enemy was tormenting and terrorizing Zachary as he fought to believe them.

It was also a constant struggle for Zachary to break free from the lie that he was no longer forgiven. The enemy convinced him that he didn't deserve forgiveness because Jesus had rescued him during the first drug-induced incident, and then he had smoked pot again.

In addition, he constantly heard the enemy repeating what he had told him during his trip to hell: he wasn't "Zachary" anymore, and his life was no longer his own. And Zachary believed it. He became completely unsure of who he was. As I said before, I would not acknowledge who the enemy told Zach he was now, especially out loud. Instead, I chose to speak only the truth of who Zachary was—and who he would become—to counteract it.

There is an important spiritual principle involved in this strategy: *the power of the spoken word*. If you look all the way back to the creation account in Genesis, you will see that God's chosen tool to create our world was the spoken word: *"And then God said…."* Even as humans, our words carry more power than we generally realize.

> *"Death and life are in the power of the tongue, and those who love it will eat its fruit"* (Proverbs 18:21).

For all appearances, Zachary seemed to be losing his mind. But the last thing we wanted was to somehow validate and empower the enemy's lies by speaking them with our mouths. God's Word is always the standard of truth, not our glaring circumstances, and I had to force my mouth to comply with this principle. I began to train Zachary to do the same. I would not allow any talk of what the enemy said to him or seemed to be saying through his symptoms. Instead, we chose to declare the truth of God's Word in its place.

Let me be clear, I knew we were under heavy spiritual attack. This was not a matter of denial. One would have needed only to visit our home for a day to know that. But instead of walking around concentrating on the devil and demons—or even rebuking them in the midst of Zachary's attacks—I chose, instead, to focus on God and His goodness. In fact, I felt strongly that God instructed me this way. I knew Zachary's focus and my focus had to be on God and *who He is*, not on the enemy and *what he was doing*. Darkness feeds on attention and fear, and I wasn't going to offer it any nourishment.

In spite of all this, Zachary still believed the enemy's lies in his heart. He didn't realize he was empowering the devil by believing his lies—because power is always bred by agreement. And that agreement was having devastating effects on him.

I am not telling you this to cause fear. I am not giving glory to demons. I understand that for some, this is a hard read. I encourage you to press through. God is indeed mighty to save. The enemy of our souls will not prevail. The attack on my son didn't prevail. I am telling you this to help you grasp and understand the tactics of the enemy. We have to learn how to wage war. And unbeknownst to me at the time, the strategy God gave me—of knowing Him *first* and knowing the truth of who we are *second*—was an absolute masterpiece.

FAITH—A POWERFUL WEAPON

As the days dragged on, we continued to pull out weapons from our spiritual arsenal to add to the divine strategy God gave me. One weapon we knew could not stay sheathed was faith, because without faith it is impossible to please Him (Hebrews 11:6). With faith, however, one can move mountains (Matthew 17:20).

As I continually dove into His Word for answers and hope to boost my faith, I was reminded of when a distraught father ran to Jesus about his dying daughter in Luke 8.

> *"So it was, when Jesus returned, that the multitude welcomed Him, for they were all waiting for Him. And behold, there came a man named Jairus, and he was a ruler of the synagogue. And he fell down at Jesus' feet and begged Him to come to his house, for he had an only daughter about twelve years of age, and she was dying. …While He was still speaking, someone came from the ruler of the synagogue's house, saying to him, "Your daughter is dead. Do not trouble the Teacher." But when Jesus heard it, He answered him, saying,* **'Do not be afraid; only believe, and she will be made well.'** *When He came into the house,* **He permitted no one to go in except Peter, James, and John, and the father and mother of the girl.** *Now all wept and mourned for her; but He said, 'Do not weep; she is not dead, but sleeping.' And* **they**

*ridiculed Him, **knowing that she was dead**. But **He put them all outside**, took her by the hand and called, saying, 'Little girl, arise.' Then her spirit returned, and she arose immediately. And He commanded that she be given something to eat. And her parents were astonished, but **He charged them to tell no one what had happened**"* (Luke 8:40-42, 49-56).

God spoke to me through His example. One of the instructions I felt I received from the Lord was to be discerning about who we shared the gravity of our situation with, until Zachary was made completely whole. God explained that the *facts of our circumstances* would be hard to ignore, and would make it difficult to have faith for Zachary's complete healing. Notice in the above verses, it says, *"they ridiculed Him, **knowing** that she was dead."*

It was indeed a fact that the daughter was dead from the world's perspective. But not, you see, from heaven's. God's love and power always trumps the "facts" of our earthly circumstances.

Keeping Zachary's condition close to our chest made sense to me. On the one hand, Richard and I were providing a covering over our son by not broadcasting this to the world or allowing a diagnosis to be stuck to him like a label. On the other hand, God was getting unbelief "out of the room" and out of our own hearts. Jesus did the same when petitioned for help by Jairus. Besides Jairus and his wife, Jesus only allowed a few men of enormous faith to be in the house with Him when ministering to their daughter.

Because of what we felt was a directive from the Lord, we only shared with a small group of mighty men and women of faith, who agreed to dress for war on our behalf. In God's kindness and wisdom, He strategically surrounded our family with a few who would stand with us in absolute faith that God alone would heal Zachary—completely.

In those first few weeks, I struggled with believing that myself. I wondered if my husband and I were doing the right thing by not taking Zachary to a doctor or a hospital. I knew that too many opinions and voices in my head were not what I needed. I needed to hear what God had to say on the matter. And the only way to hear God in the midst of the chaos was to quiet as many other voices as I could.

Those we enlisted in battle agreed to pray that Zachary would not simply *get better* and come through this a *survivor*, but that he would walk out completely whole and a mighty warrior on the other side.

Choosing to tell some and not others wasn't because our other friends didn't have faith or could not be trusted. Many of the people I kept this from were ones who loved Zachary deeply and who would have prayed in faith for us intently. And I knew that. Not telling some of my dearest friends and family was one of the hardest things I have ever done, and it proved lonely at times. But I had to obey, though I didn't fully understand.

Looking back now, one of the things God was doing in this was ridding me of relying too heavily on people. Yes, I still relied on the friends we enlisted in many ways. But ever so gently, by removing the rest, God was weaning me off my trust in man and putting my faith where it belonged—in Him alone.

A BOOK OF REMEMBRANCE

When you are going through a dark time, one side effect can be to forget the power and the goodness of God. When God isn't doing what you think He should, it is easy to focus on the problem, and it suddenly becomes larger than the solution—which is God Himself. The enemy can appear to be stronger than he actually is and more powerful than God Almighty. And when the enemy becomes our focus, even unwittingly, he receives glory. Doubt seeps in as to God's kindness, as well. I could see this happening in my own heart, and it disturbed me.

God began to reveal a way to turn our hearts back toward the goodness and power of God. It became another key to our breakthrough: to remember.

Richard and I began to call to remembrance and remind Zachary of God's love made evident in our individual experiences. We shared with him past stories of God's intervention in our personal lives and in the lives of our family, even going back long before he was born and we were married. We began to do this daily. We weren't simply reminding *our son* of the strength and love of our God, we were remembering and reminding *ourselves*. And it began to spread a new fire in our hearts.

Eventually, what we expressed verbally through this dark season became tangible. What poured forth from our hearts as a means of strategy morphed into a family journal. As each of us shared, I recorded things we were thankful to God for, over the course of our lifetimes. It wasn't an exhaustive list by any stretch, but we wanted to do something special to commemorate God's mighty acts on our behalf.

We decided on a "Smeltzer Book of Remembrance." It contained things like special relationships God had blessed us with, adventures we had gone on and the favor we had experienced individually and as a family. It also spoke of the provision we had received, both in times of lack and in times of plenty. We documented times of God's divine protection and rescue. We acknowledged the areas where we had received God's grace and mercy. We wrote of the miracles God had done for us personally, and the miracles we were blessed to witness in the lives of the people we love. We documented everything we could think of, as a tribute to God's goodness and His love toward us.

It all started when I read Nehemiah 9, in reference to God's mercy. This excellent chapter recounts many of the amazing acts God performed for the Israelites, especially in bringing them out of their slavery in Egypt. Verses 16-17 say, "***But** they and our fathers acted presumptuously and stiffened their neck and did not obey your commandments. They refused to obey and **were not mindful of the wonders that you performed among them**, but they stiffened their neck and appointed a leader to return to their slavery in Egypt. But you are a God ready to forgive, gracious and merciful, slow to anger and abounding in steadfast love, and did not forsake them*" (ESV).

When I read these two verses, something jumped out at me... *"they were not mindful of His wonders."* I looked up the word "mindful" in the original Hebrew. It means "to call to remembrance" and "to make a memorial."

The Israelites hadn't been mindful of His wonders. And I hadn't been, either. I was quick to be mindful of what God was *not* doing. *That*, I had no problem with. I had a list of unanswered prayers—especially concerning Zachary—always at the forefront of my mind, and yet I was failing to call to remembrance what God *had* so mercifully and powerfully done in the past on my behalf, and on behalf of my children and loved ones.

We began to learn during this season that *remembering*—with an attitude of thankfulness—is a powerful tool against the enemy. God began to teach me about being intentional each day, not only to remember what God *had done* for us in the past, but to celebrate what He *was doing* in the present. It was a deliberate act of my will to pay attention to what God was doing and to be thankful. This was difficult, because it often felt like nothing was changing. But I learned that it was important—even another weapon—not only to acknowledge, but also to celebrate "small" miracles or the baby steps Zachary was making toward healing. This intentionality encouraged a spirit of gratitude in our hearts, which gave birth to hope. And hope, my friends, does not disappoint! (Romans 5:5)

NOW WHAT? HOW CAN I RESPOND?

1. Are you or someone you know experiencing something similar? Or are you suffering hard circumstances and asking why? First things first: It is always wise to "check-in" with yourself and see if you are allowing anything into your life and heart that may be leaving you vulnerable to attack. There are the obvious ways like drugs and sexual sin, but a huge open door can simply be unforgiveness in your heart.

2. Close any doors you may have opened through sin and disobedience by repenting and asking God's forgiveness, through the blood of Jesus. You may even need to go to another person and ask forgiveness, if the sin or unforgiveness involves them. Allow His blood to wash over and cleanse you. Make a conscious choice, through faith and the power of His Holy Spirit, to walk away from the sin. Remember, repentance is doing a 180-degree turn. You may need help with this. Transparency and vulnerability are powerful weapons. When we are weak, He is strong. There is no shame in asking for help, as Zachary did (see 2 Corinthians 12:9-10).

   Keep in mind: sometimes an accusing spirit can lie to us after a time of repentance, causing us to struggle to believe and accept God's forgiveness. This usually results in one of two things. The first is fear and despair—because the heart doesn't truly believe it deserves forgiveness. This is what happened to

Zachary. I had to encourage him with the truth of God's Word, daily, to combat it.

*"If we confess our sins, He is **faithful and just** to forgive us our sins **and** to cleanse us from all unrighteousness"* (1 John 1:9).

The second is that a religious spirit can set in that causes you to try to *earn* your salvation and forgiveness by determining—in your own strength—to *be good*, thereby choosing performance over walking in the power of His Spirit. Both of these are lies. We are only saved through faith, because of the blood of Jesus shed for us. Period. We cannot work for our forgiveness and salvation. They are free gifts.

"For by grace you have been saved through faith. And this is not your own doing; it is the gift of God, not a result of works, so that no one may boast" (Ephesians 2:8-9, ESV).

3. Have you already covered these bases, yet still have no relief? Ask God for a strategy. The one God gave me is a great start. It is my personal opinion that the best strategy on earth, to combat the enemy of our souls, is to know the truth of who God is and to know the truth of who He says we are. Pray and ask God to reveal Himself to you afresh and to teach you who you are in Him. Begin to study His attributes, His names and His character, as revealed in the Bible.

(See the Bonus Section at the back of the book. It contains a Devotional, guides to help you, and a list of scriptures revealing God's names, nature and character. You will also find a list of scriptures stating who God says we are in Christ. These lists are by no means exhaustive, but they are a good start.)

4. Ask God to reveal what lies you believe about Him and about yourself. Your expectation of His movement in your life will give you clues as to your real beliefs about who He is. Ask Him to show you the places where what Scripture says and the true beliefs of your heart are in conflict. We all have those places where we have allowed our experience and our circumstances to dictate who He is over the truth of His Word.

   (If only Adam and Eve had done this before eating the forbidden fruit! If only they had gone to God with their questions about why He didn't want them eating the fruit, instead of assuming—via the enemy's planted lies—that God's intentions toward them were not for their good, but an act of withholding. This same lie is common today. We see God as *taking something from us* in the very places He is actually *giving a blessing to us*.)

5. Repent and choose to come out of agreement with these lies, by faith.

6. Replace the lies with the truth of God's Word. By faith, choose to come into agreement with who He says He is. Meditate on these truths. Feed on them. Declare them, out loud, in faith—no matter how long it takes. Sometimes it takes our hearts time to catch up with our words. It actually took about a year or more for Zachary, but his heart eventually caught up to what his mind chose to feed on.

"Finally, brethren, whatever things are true, whatever things are noble, whatever things are just, whatever things are pure, whatever things are lovely, whatever things are of

good report, if there is any virtue and if there is anything praiseworthy—meditate on these things" (Philippians 4:8).

7. When the enemy comes and plays the old recordings in your head, telling you lies about who God is and who you are, be diligent to take every thought captive. Yes, often what we think is our own thoughts and negative self-talk is actually a lying spirit. Grab the lie, so to speak. Call the enemy a liar. Speak the truth of what God says in place of the enemy's lies. Continue to choose to embrace the truth found in His Word. Declare that your heart will believe and embrace the Truth (this is what Jesus did when tempted by satan in the wilderness).

"For the weapons of our warfare are not carnal but mighty in God for pulling down strongholds, casting down arguments and every high thing that exalts itself against the knowledge of God, bringing every thought into captivity to the obedience of Christ" (2 Corinthians 10:4-5).

8. "Watch your mouth." Be aware of the power of your spoken words. Be intentional to speak what is truth—from God's Word and His perspective—and not the "facts" of your circumstances that do not agree.

9. Establish an atmosphere of faith by "getting unbelief out of the room." Find people who will agree to battle with you, in faith, for your complete victory.

PRAYER

Dear Lord, I pray You would begin to take me on an adventure of discovering—afresh—who You are. I pray You would begin to break down any lies that have become structures in my heart. I ask that You would silence any voices I hear—any recordings playing in my head—that are not speaking the truth about who You are, or about who I am in Your sight. I pray You would dispel the lies I believe about You, even those I'm not even aware of yet. I thank You, knowing You will reveal these in Your timing and in Your love.

I pray You would begin to heal the deepest parts of me: places I have been traumatized, discouraged and left hopeless. In the places where I don't see Your hand coming in to heal me and rescue me—or those I love—enable me to hope again.

Renew my hope in Your love and goodness. I thank You for being a good Father, with plans to bless me and not to harm me, to give me a future and a hope.

Give me a gift of faith, Lord, so I can come to believe with confidence for You to be ***all*** You are: in me, for me and through me. In Jesus' name, Amen!

CHAPTER THREE

Stepping Through Offense

And blessed is he who is not offended because of Me.
~Jesus of Nazareth (Matthew 11:6)

LOOKING BACK NOW, I see that the strategy God gave me was working from the very first day. But at the time, it felt like quite the opposite. From my vantage point, it looked like demons had taken up residence in my home to torture my son and, no matter how I kept to the strategy, they were allowed to stay. I fought with everything in me, until I fell into fits of exhaustion. At times, I even cried and screamed out to God until unimaginable sounds bubbled up out of the depth of my soul. If God's strategy was working, it wasn't happening fast enough for my taste.

Zachary walked around day after day with a tortured, lifeless look in his eyes. He never showed joy in anything. He never laughed. He rarely smiled. If he did, the smile was forced for my and Richard's benefit. It was as if his very life was being sucked out of him, and he was becoming a shell. Yet he continued walking painstakingly forward, one foot in front of the other toward the Lord.

As an act of faith, Zachary requested to be baptized by our

missionary friend on Sunday, August 21st, even though he had been baptized earlier as a young boy. At this point, we were only three weeks into this and it already felt like years. Zachary believed with all his heart that the attacks would stop once he made an outward commitment reflecting the inward one he had experienced in his heart. We, too, felt this would be the breakthrough he needed. Out of love for our son, our friend and his wife flew in from California to honor Zach's request.

Not only did Zachary's attacks fail to stop after his baptism, but they actually intensified. My 18-year-old son, always brave in the past, asked me to start sleeping in his room due to horrific nightmares that began nightly. The nightmares came in the form of a bear attacking him, ripping his legs off and leaving him bleeding. He would hold my hand and clutch it to his heart as he slept. Before falling asleep each night, Zach asked me to read scripture to him, to pray for him and to remind him of God's love and promises.

We were about three weeks into this nightmare when Zachary began seeing things and having vision problems. We took him to an eye doctor, who found nothing. In the midst of all of this, my faith was challenged more than I ever thought possible. I encouraged myself by remembering Jesus' own baptism. He, too, was then led into the wilderness for 40 days to be tempted and tormented by the devil. So *surely* this would not go on past 40 days for my son.

Funny how we do that to God, isn't it? We try to figure Him out, put restrictions on Him, and tell Him what He can and can't do in our lives. We draw a line in the sand and *ask* Him not to cross it. Back then, I think my heart was demanding it. I showed Him His own Word in scripture and tried to convince Him it could be no other way.

The problem was that I was looking through the eyes of my own understanding, and it appeared our acts of faith were producing nothing. I knew this could not be true. I had walked with God long enough to know that any attempt to twist His arm was unnecessary, at best—because as His daughter, I have His ear and because faith *always* bears fruit. But God was doing a deeper work of teaching me to stand firm and trust, even when He appeared not to be listening. Even when He appeared silent. Even when He appeared to be going against His own promises.

As the battle between my spirit and my flesh continued, I reminded myself that it may not look like you expect—or come when you expect it to—but faith *always* produces a crop. It has to. God established a law of sowing and reaping, so it can be no other way. True, sometimes it takes a long time to see it, and sometimes what you thought you planted isn't exactly what breaks forth from the ground, but it comes nonetheless. For Zachary, and for me as well, seeds were sprouting deep below the surface, but they would remain unseen for what seemed like an eternity.

In the meantime, the horror film I was seeing played out on the screen of my life continued to vie for my attention. Zach ended up quitting his job because he couldn't cope. He started his senior year of high school the beginning of September. He would leave class and call me from his car, crying. He couldn't even make the 15-minute drive home. I would have to pick him up and leave his car at school. When he didn't have to be at school, he still wouldn't leave the house without us. He would have 43 absences and tardies by the end of the school year. And it all felt like a bad dream. Scrap that. It felt like a nightmare, and I couldn't wake up.

The truth is, I was beyond weary. I was mad. Not with the enemy, although I was angry with him, too. In all honesty, I was angry at God. I wasn't even aware of it at first. Then I didn't want to admit it, even to myself. Finally, I got plain honest and told God I was ticked off at Him. I remember thinking, "I thought we were friends. I thought you loved me!" I am not even sure I used nice words. He was not being the God I knew. He wasn't acting according to His Word, or so I thought, and I let Him know it.

Yes, this was my distorted perception at the time. I knew God doesn't cause the bad things that happen to us. Sometimes the enemy does, but much of what we go through is a result of living in a fallen world. In His great love for us, God gave mankind free will. He keeps His promise by not violating it. Consequently, one wrong choice can have a domino effect—even on a nation. If God moved us around like chess pieces at His every whim, we would be His slaves—not His beloved children. Still, we often become offended when God doesn't fix things our way or according to our timetable.

God certainly wasn't fixing my son according to *my* timetable. And I was quick to tell Him so. Oh, I still loved Him. I loved Him fiercely, and I knew He loved me. I've known that since the day I met Him as a 15-year-old girl. But I just wanted this all to stop. I knew God had the power to make it stop, and He wasn't complying. I pleaded with Him incessantly, yet it seemed to fall on deaf ears.

As I said before, I'm a *logic girl*, and it made no sense. My friends tease me that I "always try to figure God out." And it's true, I do! I have had to work hard to embrace the mystery. I am learning that I don't need to know everything up front, and that I can trust God in the process—in the waiting. I am learning to walk in peace when I don't understand with my mind. But at the time, all I wanted was answers. I was desperate for them. And I wanted them now!

I SIMPLY DON'T APPROVE!

We were about a month and a half into this with Zach when I journaled the following…

Today is September 15th and it has continued. We have seen glimpses of hope and peace. Yet they have remained glimpses. The battle has been just as much for my husband and me as for our son. Especially for me, his mother. It seems that every time the attack is the worst, Richard is either at work, the grocery store or on some errand. When I asked the Lord why I was always alone to deal with the brunt of it, as it is terrifying, God answered, "Because this is your demon to battle, too." I am guessing this is because I have battled fear since I was a child. And it seems to be a generational issue.

I have suffered many trials in my life, but my Momma's heart says, "Not my son!" I have battled fear and despair and even anger at my God for allowing such a thing that seems to go against His very Word, His character and His name. It goes against all I know God to be. He says, "Resist the devil and he will flee from you." Zach is resisting with everything in him yet the devil doesn't seem to be fleeing. God says, "Those the Son sets free are free indeed." Zachary has repented, accepted Him, worshipped Him, and sought Him for freedom, yet he seems to be in bondage, regardless. God's Word says, "He resists the proud, but gives grace to the humble." I have seen my son walk in tremendous humility, yet I have not seen God's grace in his circumstances. I could quote scriptures all day long, yet God doesn't seem to be living or acting according to His own words.

And yet…

I am reminded of Peter when Jesus spoke a very offensive message to a large crowd—one that sent them packing. He told them in John 6 that they must "eat His flesh and drink His blood" to have life. He offended the masses—intentionally and without explanation. "From that time many of His disciples went back and walked with Him no more. Then Jesus said to the twelve, 'Do you also want to go away?' But Simon Peter answered Him, 'Lord, to whom shall we go? You have the words of eternal life.'"

In spite of offense—though it seemed that Jesus was speaking in complete opposition to the scriptures—Peter remained. His response? "Where else would I go? Only You have the words of life." I feel Him asking me the same, "Kristen, do you also want to go away?" My only answer—my only hope—is in Him. Where else would I go?

And there it is…I was offended. Granted, I was pushing through it, but I was offended. I knew God was my *only* hope, but I was hurt and angry, and I wasn't afraid to express it anymore.

In my heart, I was saying, "I suffered through the difficult trials that have happened to me. But *this is MY SON! Don't you understand? This is MY SON!*"

Forget for a moment the irony and pure audacity of my question; in truth, my accusation. Of course God knew what it was like to watch His Son suffer at the hands of the enemy. He watched His Son suffer unto death, the worst death imaginable. But I was a mother in anguish over her son. Zachary appeared to be losing his mind right before my eyes, and I knew God was the only one with the power to make him whole. And I tried everything I could to make Him use it.

At times I must have sounded like a spoiled child throwing a temper tantrum. Did He strike me dead? Chastise me for my sharp tongue? On the contrary. He was so kind, now that I look back on it. He knew my pain. He knew my love for my son. And He listened. It felt like deafening silence. But truth be told, He was always there—always instilling truth and love in my heart. His kindness is what got me through.

WHEN GOD OFFENDS—ON PURPOSE

Jesus is indeed a stumbling block. He has been from the beginning. His message brings offense. For example, when you are knee-deep in sin—and loving it—the last thing you want to hear is a message of holiness. This, I get. I can wrap my mind around it and make some sense of it all. When you are engrossed in willful sin, Jesus is offensive.

When you are doing your best to honor and obey Him, however, you can falsely assume you are past being offended by Him. Convicted, yes. Disciplined in love, of course. But not offended. The real shocker for me was—when I whole-heartedly sought Him in my darkest hour—He not only allowed me to be offended, but He purposely pushed me into it. He didn't rush in to save the day. He offered no explanation of our suffering. He revealed no end in sight. He simply allowed Himself to appear contrary to all I know of Him—and waited for my response.

Remember my journal entry about Jesus offending the crowd in John 6? Jesus had been talking to 5,000 followers in this section of scripture (they are called "disciples" in this text, but He isn't addressing His twelve disciples until verse 67).

Let's look at it more closely in John 6:53-61…

"Then Jesus said to them, 'Most assuredly, I say to you, unless you eat the flesh of the Son of Man and drink His blood, you have no life in you. Whoever eats My flesh and drinks My blood has eternal life, and I will raise him up at the last day. For My flesh is food indeed, and My blood is drink indeed. He who eats My flesh and drinks My blood abides in Me, and I in him. As the living Father sent Me, and I live because of the Father, so he who feeds on Me will live because of Me. This is the bread which came down from heaven—not as your fathers ate the manna, and are dead. He who eats this bread will live forever.' These things He said in

the synagogue as He taught in Capernaum. Therefore many of His disciples, when they heard this, said, 'This is a hard saying; who can understand it?' When Jesus knew in Himself that His disciples complained about this, He said to them, **'Does this offend you?'"**

Here He asks the question, "Does this offend you?" Of course it did! And Jesus knew it full well. In their minds His statements suggested cannibalism—to eat His flesh and drink His blood—an abomination to the Jews. He could have explained that He was speaking metaphorically, yet He chose not to.

If you keep reading on, verse 66 says,

"From that time many of His disciples went back and walked with Him no more."

Many of His disciples left at this point because of the offense Jesus seemed to cause—on purpose! He had a crowd of about 5,000 following Him. That's a nice-sized church. Yet He *still* doesn't clarify Himself and put their minds at ease to keep them around. So much for "seeker sensitive."

Instead of giving the inside scoop to His chosen twelve He continues in verses 67-69…

"Then Jesus said to the twelve, **'Do you also want to go away?'** *But Simon Peter answered Him,* **'Lord, to whom shall we go? You have the words of eternal life.** *Also we have come to believe and know that You are the Christ, the Son of the living God.'"*

Here, Jesus purposely offended the twelve disciples, His closest friends and followers—those He was mentoring to become the foundation of His church. He forced the issue—either walk away or believe—regardless of what made sense to their rational minds. Regardless of their logic. It doesn't seem to bother Jesus in the slightest that, for all appearances sake, He contradicted His own Word. Why does Jesus do this? Why does He come as an offense? It sure doesn't fall into the category of "How to win friends and influence people!"

There are several reasons, and I will list more thoughts on this later. But in the above section of scripture when Jesus tells the crowd they must eat His flesh and drink His blood, Jesus was purposely bypassing their intellect—even their perfect theology—to get to their hearts, to get to their spirits. Jesus constantly spoke in mysteries and parables. It was up to the people to seek out the meaning.

God does this with me often. It makes me laugh, now, thinking of some of the things He has said to me—seemingly for shock value. More than once I have initially taken offense at His words and then pondered it—only to realize how He was actually loving me through them. If you are willing to have ears to hear what He is saying, He will captivate your heart with His mysteries of love.

That is what Jesus was doing with this message. It was a mystery of love. When addressing the crowd, Jesus gave them something to chew on. All it seemed to do was cause a bad taste in their mouths. But God knows the hearts of man. He was not concerned about their momentary decision to walk away. Why?

On the one hand, though God is "*not willing that any should perish but that all should come to repentance*" (2 Peter 3:9), He allows each one a choice to walk away. And He will never demand our belief or affection. But on the other hand, Jesus also knew that *any who had a heart for truth* would walk away for a season, but would remember what He said as they watched Jesus hang on a cross. They would remember His words and have their "Aha!" moment when they saw Him risen.

They would realize He was speaking of embracing and personally accepting His sacrifice on the cross—His flesh and His blood—for their salvation. *Those who had ears to hear* would eventually realize He was the long-awaited Messiah, who came to die for the sins of the world. Therefore, Jesus was patient with their process of discovery. He knew that once these stepped through their offense, they would find eternal life on the other side.

Proverbs 25:2 teaches,

> *"It is the glory of God to conceal a matter, but the glory of kings is to search out a matter."*

God calls us to be His *"kings and priests"* in Revelation 1:6. Therefore, He is training us to "search out a matter." He speaks in mysteries to train us to listen to His Holy Spirit with our spirit, and not rely only on our soul (our mind, will and emotions) for truth. It is in the seeking that we find and become strengthened in Him. The exercise of searching Him out is part of our process of discovery. And that journey develops our spiritual muscle.

> *"God is **Spirit**, and those who worship Him must worship **in spirit and truth**"* (John 4:24).

God is not man that He can be fully understood with the mind. Trust me, I have tried. He is Spirit. And we need His Holy Spirit to guide us into all truth. Thankfully, He promises us just that (see John 16:13).

Jesus is after this training in all of us—that we listen with our spirits, connected to His Holy Spirit. I am not saying we don't need to know scripture or can give up being rooted in the Word of truth. We are to be transformed by the renewing of our minds through the washing of the Word (Ephesians 5:26 and Romans 12:2). But God wants that truth to go deeper than strengthening our soul. He wants us to know Him so intimately that we recognize Him with our spirits, even when He doesn't make sense—and even offends our natural minds.

What parent doesn't want their child to grow up healthy and strong? Muscles are strengthened through resistance. And as He was clearly doing in my weakness, God is always developing our spiritual muscle through the resistance we encounter.

His Word promises we will have trials and tribulations in this life. Often, however, we strive for "the path of least resistance" when everything around us is happiness and bliss. That is because we have often mistaken the seasons of ease in our lives for God's blessing. God *has* blessed us, but what we don't understand is that sometimes He is blessing us even more when everything appears to be falling apart at the seams. Why? Because in these seasons, God is building something in us that is eternal.

The enemy of our souls is out to kill, steal and destroy us. And God is training us to recognize Him and to hear His voice—especially in our darkest nights. He is training us for war.

> *"Blessed be the* Lord *my Rock,*
> *Who trains my hands for war,*
> *And my fingers for battle—*
> *My lovingkindness and my fortress,*
> *My high tower and my deliverer,*
> *My shield and the One in whom I take refuge,*
> *Who subdues my people under me.*
>
> Lord, *what is man, that You take knowledge of him?*

> *Or the son of man, that You are mindful of him?*
> ***Man is like a breath;***
> ***His days are like a passing shadow"***

(Psalm 144:1-4).

If we can truly wrap our minds around the fact that heaven is real and our time on earth is but a passing shadow, then our lives—no matter how long they are in years—are simply a *training day* for eternity. And I, for one, want to be strong and proven valiant in battle when my day is done.

LEFT TO ROT

One lie Zach seemed to struggle with during this season was how strong satan appeared to be—how much power he seemed to have over him. When our focus is on the enemy and all he is doing, we can lose sight of the vast greatness and power of God. Unconsciously, we let God seem minimized and impotent in our minds.

This causes a snowball effect that touches our identity to the core, because if God isn't who He said He is, how can we be who He says we are? If God is callous to our pain, what hope do we have in perilous times? If God is impotent, how can we walk in any power and authority as His children—as kings and priests of the Most High God? What hope do we really have if God isn't who He said He is?

John the Baptist must have felt the same. If anyone knew who Jesus was—besides His mother Mary—it was John. John knew Jesus from the womb. John leapt in his mother's womb when Jesus entered the room in Mary's womb. When Jesus came to John to be baptized (in John 1:29), John said, "Behold! The Lamb of God who takes away the sin of the world!" Only God can take away sin, and John knew it. This statement was declaring Jesus as the Jews' long-awaited Messiah. Yet there sat John, left alone in a prison to rot, and Jesus wasn't doing a thing about it. Maybe he was wrong about Him?

> *"Now it came to pass, when Jesus finished commanding His twelve disciples, that He departed from there to teach and to preach in their cities. And when John had heard in prison about the works of Christ, he sent two of his disciples and said to Him, 'Are You the Coming One, or do we look for another?'"* (Matthew 11:1-3)

In verse 3, John sent messengers to Jesus to question His deity. *"Are You the Coming One, or do we look for another?"* I get this! Don't you? John had based his whole life on the fact Jesus was the Messiah. And yet here he was, Jesus' cousin no less, stuck in a prison cell. Didn't Jesus know? Didn't He have the ability and power to set him free? Didn't Jesus love him enough to do something? Maybe He wasn't who John thought He was, after all. And if not, John was doomed!

How does Jesus answer John's question? Jesus doesn't tell John what he wants to hear, that is for sure. He doesn't tell him: "Hey! I haven't forgotten you. I know you are in prison, and I am on my way to get you out." He basically tells John he is focused on the wrong thing.

Jesus sent a message back to John in Matthew 11:4-6:

> *"Go and tell John the things which you hear and see: The blind see and the lame walk; the lepers are cleansed and the deaf hear; the dead are raised up and the poor have the gospel preached to them.* ***And blessed is he who is not offended because of Me.****"*

In other words, Jesus was saying, "Don't allow My identity to be based on what I am *not* doing. Base it on what I *am* doing. Base it on *who I AM*."

Christa Black Gifford says, "If you are not anchored in the goodness of God, you will lower your theology to match your pain." When Jesus said, "Blessed is He who is not offended because of Me," He was basically saying, "Blessed is he who can be stuck in the prison of his circumstances and still believe in the truth of Who I Am. That I am ALWAYS good. That I am ALWAYS love. That I am ALWAYS all-powerful. That I am ALWAYS working behind the scenes doing something amazing!"

That's hard to do, isn't it? If we do some soul searching, we will find we do the same. We look at the circumstances of our life and make untrue determinations of God as a result.

I believe God would also say... "blessed is he who can be stuck in the prison of his own circumstances and still believe in the truth of who I say *he* is." In times of trial, who we are will always be tested, too.

"IT'S YOUR DEMON TO BATTLE, TOO."

In my journal entry, I expressed that one of the reasons I was offended with God is the fact I felt alone in dealing with this. It is true my husband is a mighty warrior and was fighting alongside me. He is a man of great faith, and I am beyond thankful for his part in what we went through. But it is also true—as Zachary would attest —Richard was absent through the worst of it.

Zachary had "episodes" when fear would come upon him with such intensity it seemed we were in the midst of a horror film. This was when Zachary would come and grab my hand, his eyes pleading for help, and I would use the strategy God gave me. *Every single* time this happened, Richard was gone. He would either be at work, at the grocery store, on a business call in the next room, or otherwise tied up.

It wasn't that Richard was emotionally unavailable. On the contrary, he was willing and able to help. But the enemy seemed to attack Zachary when he and I were most vulnerable. When the strength of my husband was out of the room, so to speak, the enemy swept in like a flood. And I noticed. Boy, did I notice.

I went before the Lord and asked why. Honestly, I am pretty sure this was another time when I was demanding He answer. "Why? Why do you allow Richard to be gone every time Zachary gets hit with the worst of this? I am weary. This is frightening! Why do You leave me alone to handle this day after day? Why is Richard never here to shoulder us?"

God did answer me. He answered me immediately. I knew it was Him, because I have learned to recognize His still small voice. It came completely out of left field and was nothing I would have ever thought of on my own. His answer? "Because it's your demon to battle, too."

As I was prone to do, I took His answer and filtered it through my logic. I decided that because I had battled fear most of my life—as did some others on my side of the family—God was allowing me to face this spirit of fear on my own, to get *out of me* whatever vestige of it was *in me*.

In truth, I was upset. I just wanted this all to end as quickly as possible. Was this the time to work on *me*? Didn't He see I was dying here? Didn't He understand I was trying to help my son? I had to be dragged through hell myself, too? And *by* myself, for that matter?

I consoled myself by figuring, "At least God will use this to rid my heart of fear." And while it's true that the trials did help me overcome fear, I assumed God was making me stand alone as a means of pulling something negative *out* of me. But I wouldn't realize until a few years later that I couldn't have been more wrong.

PRINCIPLE OF BLESSING

"My brethren, count it all joy when you fall into various trials, knowing that the testing of your faith produces patience. But let patience have its perfect work, that you may be perfect and complete, lacking nothing" (James 1:2-4).

God says we are to face our trials and testing by *"counting it all joy."* I am sure you have realized by now that I was not facing mine with a big "YIPPEE!" I wanted it over, and over now. I didn't care about *"patience having its perfect work."* God had always been my strong tower and mighty defense. Now—when I needed Him most—He appeared to be sleeping on the job, and I continued to shake Him, trying to awaken Him from His slumber.

Unbeknownst to me, God was dreaming of how He would bless me, of how He would bless my son, and of all His plans to turn our mourning into dancing. Because, you see, God has no problem pushing us into offense and a crisis of our faith. Why? For a blessing on the other side.

We can find evidence of God purposely offending and a resulting blessing throughout the Bible. Elijah offended the widow by asking for her and her child's last meal—imagine the audacity—and then her food never ran out. Elijah also offended the man who came to be healed of leprosy by telling him to dip in a filthy river, and then the man was healed when he complied. Jesus spit in the dirt and wiped the resulting mud on a blind man's eyes—yuck! And then he received his sight. Jesus told the rich man to sell everything he had and follow Him, and the man walked away sad. *If only* he had pushed through his offense to the reward on the other side!

God does the same with us. He pushes us to offense—without

explanation—and asks us the same question Jesus asked His disciples, "Do you also want to go away?" And then we have a choice. We either believe, or we don't. We either let Him be God, or we put Him in a box. We either become discouraged and attribute evil to Him, or we trust Him with what we don't understand and choose to lock onto hope like a pit bull. We either have faith for God to restore all that the locusts have eaten in our lives—in incredible, miraculous ways—or we resign ourselves to survival and simply "arriving to heaven having been faithful in the small things." But I'm not meant for survival. I was created for victory! And you were, too!

WHY DOES GOD PUSH US INTO OFFENSE?

I believe there are several reasons. Some of them are:

- To reveal the places in our hearts where we don't fully understand His character and His ways, so we can become more grounded in the truth of who He is.
- To rid us of relying on our logic and what our minds can comprehend and to listen to His Holy Spirit.
- To expose weaknesses in our faith and make them our strengths.
- To get us to seek out His mysteries of love as He takes us from glory to glory as His kings and priests.
- To push us to a place of decision, where we must choose to believe in His goodness when we don't understand, and trust Him when we don't "approve" of what He allows in our lives.
- To get us to push in for more. God has more for our lives than we can hope to accomplish in our own strength and in accordance to our time frame. He has designed us for greatness. But to get there, we must push through the resistance of our offenses with Him, concerning our "here and now" circumstances.

- To strengthen our spiritual muscle and prepare us for eternity, because this life on earth is simply a "training day."
- To make us unoffendable. The more unoffendable we are, the more peace we have regardless of our circumstances, and the more established we are in our faith and understanding of who God is.
- To make us overcomers and to bring glory to Him.
- Finally, because our blessing—and our destiny—is often found on the other side of the walls of our offenses!

YES, I'M OFFENDED

You can probably relate on some level. God has allowed hardships in your life, and the lives of those you love, that you never dreamed you'd have to walk through. You have experienced pain, loss and death, in different—if not all—areas of your life. And as a result, you may have died to a dream, a calling or a belief in what your life was supposed to be like. You may have wondered what you have done wrong or if God is upset with you. Or maybe you are to the point that you don't care if He is. Maybe you doubt His very love for you—or at least question His goodness.

In these places in our lives, we have entered into offense with God. Like John the Baptist, we believe Jesus to be all-powerful and always good, *until* we are left alone in a prison. We believe until the truths in God's Word don't seem to work for us. Then we build a theology around our experience, or lack thereof, and create a God who can be managed and understood by our minds. Then we question His goodness and power and reduce Him to our intellect. We question the truth of Who He is.

The cost of believing God to be as huge and incomprehensible as

He is seems too much to bear, so we put Him in boxes of comfort. We reduce our theology of God to match the "facts" of our circumstances, *instead of* the truth of who He is. In our hearts, we have tamed The Lion and cut off His mane. In other words, we not only question His love for us, but His power as well.

But I am here to tell you that no matter what your circumstances, God doesn't change. Even when He seems to be asleep or acting completely against His own Word, His power and love remain and are at work in your life. He has a plan for you, and it is for *good*. It is for a hope and a future for your life. He desires for you to go on the adventure of discovering Him. His Word says He takes us from glory to glory. And His Word is truth—even more true than the "facts" staring you in the face (see 2 Corinthians 3:18).

> *"For I know the thoughts that I think toward you, says the* LORD, *thoughts of peace and not of evil, to give you a future and a hope. Then you will call upon Me and go and pray to Me, and I will listen to you. And you will seek Me and find Me, when you search for Me with all your heart"* (Jeremiah 29:11-13).

God is asking you, as He asked His disciples, "Does this offend you? Do you also wish to walk away?" He is waiting for your response. He is waiting to hear you say, "Where else would I go? Only You have the words of life."

NOW WHAT?

1. God is gentle and kind. He is inviting you into a conversation with Him. Imagine God/Jesus sitting with you as you begin, having a face-to-face chat. REMEMBER: God will always be kind and loving. If you hear anything else, stop and pray again.

Ask the Holy Spirit to quiet any spirit not of Him, and for you to only hear His voice of truth and love.

2. Be honest with Him. Tell Him the places where you have felt let down, discouraged, abandoned, rejected, afraid and even angry with Him. It is okay to be honest. He already knows your heart. Isaiah 30:18 tells us, He is the Lord who "*will wait, that He may be gracious to you.*"

3. The Holy Spirit may begin to reveal areas in your heart where you have become offended with God or where, because of pain or disappointment, you have not believed in the truth of His goodness, faithfulness or love.

4. Ask Him to show you where He was in the events that brought you to this place. If it involves trauma, ask Him to wash the trauma off of you and to cleanse the wound with His blood. Ask Him to show you, in your mind's eye, where He was in the midst of your pain. Dialogue with Him. He desires to bring healing and restoration. Keeping a journal can help you on this journey.

5. As your offenses are brought to the light, begin to lay them at His feet. Sometimes we need to "forgive" God, and voice it. Let me clarify that this isn't because God has sinned against us, but rather *we feel that way*. We don't understand what God has done or is doing, so we feel like He has treated us wrongly. "Forgiving" Him is actually releasing the pain caused by the perceived wrong. It is your choosing. He will not force you. Keep in mind that this is for you, not for Him. In truth, He never hurts us or causes us pain. The enemy does. People do. It is often our limited perspective that makes us attribute our pain to God. He doesn't need our forgiveness, but offering Him

forgiveness breaks chains *in us*. It opens our heart to receive His forgiveness and tenderness that was there all the time.

6. As God reveals the places in your heart where you are offended with Him, repent and ask His forgiveness for specific things He brings to mind. Repent for areas where you have attributed wrongdoing to Him. Ask Him to wash away the offenses under His blood, and to replace them with a deeper love *for Him*, and a gift of faith *in Him*. As an act of faith, hand Him back your heart. Trust Him to give you the gift of renewed hope and trust.

7. Declare that on the other side of these offenses is a blessing. Even more, on the other side is *your destiny*! You may not see it today. You may not see it this year. But I promise you, if you keep waiting and watching, you will. You have *not* blown the gifts and callings He has promised you. For the Bible says, *"The gifts and the calling of God are irrevocable"* (Romans 11:29) and even *"if we are faithless, He remains faithful; He cannot deny Himself" (2 Timothy 2:13)*. He can never cease to be all He is—in us, through us and for us.

SAMPLE PRAYER OF REPENTANCE

Lord, I have been offended with You. I've believed You are not loving me or those I care about well. I've falsely assumed You're not keeping Your Word. I've attributed wrongdoing to You when You haven't acted in a way I want, expect or hope. At times I've even spoken to You harshly, whether verbally or in my thoughts. And in so doing, I've been prideful, dishonoring, and have judged You falsely.

And in falsely judging You, I've elevated myself. I've made myself out to be more loving than You. And I'm wrong. Nothing could be further from the truth. I repent for the places in my heart where I've chosen to listen to the enemy instead of You. I've looked at my circumstances and let them dictate who You are, and I've minimized You in the process. I repent for my untrue thoughts *toward* You and my untrue beliefs *of* You. Lord, would You please forgive me?

I choose, by faith, to receive Your forgiveness. I choose to believe in Your love, Your power, Your goodness, and Your plans for a hope and a future for me. I ask You to create in me a clean heart, and to renew a right spirit in me. Teach me, afresh, the truth of who You are and who You created me to be in You. Lord, give me a gift of faith and help me to lock onto hope with greater confidence and unwavering perseverance, knowing You are worthy of my faith, hope and love.

I declare that Your love and power surpasses any other, including mine. I declare that You are all-loving, all-powerful and completely good. You can never, at any moment, cease from being the Great I AM. I give you back control of my life and the lives of my loved ones, knowing we are in the most powerful and loving hands. Where else would I go, Lord? Only You have the words of life. I choose to stay. I choose YOU! Amen.

CHAPTER FOUR

It's All In A Name

What comes into our minds when we think about God is the most important thing about us.

~A. W. Tozer

Do you remember quoting the old childhood saying, "Sticks and stones may break my bones, but names will never hurt me?" I do. Who were we kidding? Names can hurt far worse. I remember a name or two spoken over me that seemed to stick to my heart like super glue. And during his trip to hell, my son had a name stuck to him that hurtled him onto a path of terror. The truth is that the power of the spoken word—or a spoken name—can take years to wash off our hearts. In the meantime, that cruel name can be limiting, to say the least. On the other hand, a name—or a name change—can transform a life.

Names were very important in scripture. They often contained a meaning that served as a declaration over the person. God reminded me of this truth while we were walking Zachary through his healing. He taught me how to incorporate the Biblical principle of a name to combat the enemy's scheme. Zachary already had a powerful given name. "Zachary" means "Jehovah has remembered," but more to the point, his full name is "Zachary David." We named him after King David while he was still in my womb because we felt God say he would have some of King David's characteristics.

When Zachary suffered these intense "episodes"—after telling him who God is—I would always start my counter-attack by reminding him of his given name. Then I would tell him who he was according to the promises in Scripture that speak to who we are in Christ. I would also tell him who he was personally: the positive and unique characteristics I saw in him, and who I believed he was destined to become.

I reminded Zachary constantly of who he was named after. King David was a mighty man who killed a bear and a lion in his youth. He went on to kill a giant with one small stone (1 Samuel 17:34-51). I would emphasize his middle name when saying, "You are Zachary *David* Smeltzer" and have him repeat it.

God instructed me to not treat Zachary based on his behavior or symptoms, but instead based on who God designed him to be. I knew that Zachary's circumstances, and even his beliefs of who he was at that point, did not define him. Only God can do that, because He is our Creator and sees the end from the beginning.

In the Bible, some were given powerful names at birth, yet at other times a name didn't fully depict who the person was or would become. Whether or not this was the reason, God changed people's names throughout scripture. The new names set their lives on a new course, often in the opposite direction.

This began with Abraham. In Genesis 17:5, we see the first name change: *"No longer shall your name be called Abram, but your name shall be Abraham; for I have made you a father of many nations."* God took Abram, meaning "lofty father," and declared him Abraham, meaning "father of a multitude." Keep in mind, God named him Abraham while he was still childless!

Another example is found in Genesis 32:28, where God said, *"Your name shall no longer be called Jacob, but Israel; for you have struggled with God and with men, and have prevailed."* Jacob's name meant "supplanter." At this point in his life, Jacob showed no signs of greatness. He simply wrestled with God for a blessing. What did God give him in response? A new name, its meaning a pronouncement: "Who prevails with God."

Name changes continued into the New Testament. Simon Bar-Jonah's name was changed to Peter. Jesus said to him, *"Blessed are you, Simon Bar-Jonah…I also say to you that you are Peter, and on this rock I will build My church, and the gates of Hades shall not prevail against it"* (Matthew 16:17-18).

Simon Bar-Jonah, meaning simply "son of Jonah," was changed to Peter, meaning "rock." Peter still denied Jesus three times, in addition to many other blunders and displays of fear. Yet God saw him as a rock, and he eventually became just that.

God didn't see Zachary as a terrified teenager. He didn't see him as the diagnosis that could have been attributed to him had we taken him to a doctor. The truth is, God doesn't see as man sees. It is a facet of His character to see people in light of who they will become, not in light of their past or even their present. God changed peoples' names long before there was proof of that potential to the naked eye. In essence, the name change was a prophetic declaration of who God created them to be—their destiny in Him.

God is called, *"the God who gives life to the dead and calls things that are not as though they were"* (Romans 4:17, NIV). This scripture is specifically referring to Abraham's name change—its contained promise and fulfillment. Another version says God, *"calls into existence the things that do not exist"* (ESV).

So what does this mean for us? I am not implying we need to go around changing our given names. This is a matter of the heart and about what we "name" each other by our words and treatment of one another. But as with all examples set by God, we are to follow in His footsteps. We are to call things that are not as though they are. The point is, we are not to give voice to one another's weaknesses and sin, and it can be a powerful tool against the enemy to declare the opposite.

As an example, when Gideon was found hiding in the winepress in Judges 6, God didn't change his given name. But instead of calling out the truth of Gideon's present weakness and sin—saying he was weak, afraid and full of doubt—God called ("named") him "O mighty man of valor." He spoke the opposite of who Gideon was presently and declared who he would become.

Sadly, many of us do just the opposite with the people around us. We call things that *were* as though *they are*. Or, things that *are* as though *they shall always be*. We even do this with those we love and those closest to us. This is the exact opposite of the heart of God.

How often do we—who are to be known by our love—attach a label to someone based on their sin, weaknesses, past, or even their present? Sometimes we go a step further. We actually keep a remembrance by *documenting* the sins and failures of people. We post it to websites, write about it in articles, forward it in emails and plaster it all over social media. And yes, even gossip about it.

We often keep a record of the *offenders* long past their repentance—when God forgot the matter. God says of Himself, *"I, even I, am He who blots out your transgressions for My own sake; And I will not remember your sins"* (Isaiah 43:25).

Keep in mind, King David in the Bible was far from perfect. David sent a man out to war and put him on the front line—with a plan for him to be killed in battle, so that David could take his wife as his own! David had already impregnated the man's wife and wanted to hide their sin of adultery. Not the kind of guy you want to bring home to Mother. Yet God loved David. He saw greatness in him. He saw a man who was after His own heart. God saw David through His eyes of love, untainted by the sins David was committing.

Don't get me wrong. God is a Holy God, and He calls us to holiness. I am not condoning, nor am I saying God condones sin. God is pure, all-encompassing, extravagant love. And yet He is Holy, and sin has to bow the knee in His presence. What I am saying is that when we sin, *God doesn't define us by it.*

When God sees each one of us, He sees a child He created. He sees us through His eyes of love. David did eventually repent. But God loved him—chose him—first, *and* even while he was knee-deep in sin. Romans 5:8 puts it this way, *"But God demonstrates His own love toward us, in that while we were still sinners, Christ died for us."*

What about us? What would we say of David if he were living today? What would we say when his back was turned to us? Would we name him "a man after God's own heart," as God did? Or would we stick the names "Murderer" and "Adulterer" to him like a scarlet letter? God says, *"As far as the east is from the west, so far has He removed our transgressions from us"* (Psalm 103:12).

I will never forget the day God drove this truth home to me. It was a few years before Zachary's situation. I had been remembering something I had done many years before, something for which I had repented at the time. As I was pondering my past sin and feeling that familiar guilt, God reprimanded me—gently, but firmly. Speaking in that still small voice, He said, *"Who are you to remember what I have forgotten?"* God was not addressing my past sin again, but instead my calling it *to my own* remembrance, when He remembered it no more!

I often think about what He told me that day. It was definitely an admonition not to label someone else according to their past or present sin. But God said this to *me* when I was recounting *my own sin.* Isn't that beautiful? This is the God we serve!

As lovers of Jesus, we ought to follow God's example and re-name people in our hearts—even when they're still in sin. Actually, especially then. We ought not to focus on others' failures and actions. Instead, we should ask God to see who each one could and will become. Then we ought to *name* each accordingly—treat each as such—now, when there is absolutely no evidence of it. If we are able to call someone what *they are not yet* as though *they already are*, we can partner with God to change the course of their life!

THE ENEMY REVEALED

God was so faithful to lay out the strategy we needed to fight alongside Zachary. I want to remind you that the strategy God gave us was for *our* battle. It is certainly duplicable, but it is not the only one. When we face battles, we must tune in to the Holy Spirit for His timely strategy. He may tell you to use all of our strategy, or only parts. Or He may give you something completely different. It depends on what you are up against. The key is to go before Him. He will tell you. I will say this, however. Knowing the truth of who God is, and knowing the truth of who you are in Him, will always be a powerful weapon of your warfare.

Our battle raged for about a year, although, thankfully, it did abate over time as we walked out the principles we'd been given. When this journey started, I went to God out of desperation and in my weakness.

It's All In A Name

When it was over, I came to Him as one who had stood with Him in battle. We were "war buddies" now, and I knew He would tell me who my enemy was.

I came before the Lord and said, "I *have* to know what that was in my home. Please tell me what demon I was dealing with." God answered me by explaining we had battled no small demon. I felt God said it was a principality of this age. Its name? "Identity Theft."

I still remember my reaction to His answer. I was honestly stunned. Remember, this was at the *end* of this long battle. Not at the beginning. The entire year, I was sure I was dealing with a spirit of fear. But God said, "Identity Theft." I think my head may have tilted to the side like a confused puppy. And then it hit me, and it hit me hard. I thought about the strategy God had given me during this battle, and it made perfect sense. I had been teaching Zachary *Who* God is, and *who* Zachary was. Both of these were about true identity!

In that moment, God also reminded me that the natural speaks of the supernatural, meaning that often what we see on earth in the natural realm speaks of what is going on in the spiritual realm. And just as identity theft was on the rise in the natural, so it was in the spiritual realm. The enemy is going after our identity, and the battle is fierce. Identity theft, as God would begin to reveal, is a common tactic of the enemy that has its roots all the way back in the Garden of Eden!

"Now the serpent was more cunning than any beast of the field which the Lord *God had made. And he said to the woman,* **"Has God indeed said,** *'You shall not eat of every tree of the garden'?" And the woman said to the serpent, "We may eat the fruit of the trees of the garden; but of the fruit of the tree which is in the midst of the garden, God has said, 'You shall not eat it, nor shall you touch it, lest you die.'" Then the serpent said to the woman, "You*

will not surely die. For God knows that in the day you eat of it your eyes will be opened, and you will be like God, knowing good and evil." So when the woman saw that the tree was good for food, that it was pleasant to the eyes, and a tree desirable to make one wise, she took of its fruit and ate. She also gave to her husband with her, and he ate" (Genesis 3:1-6).

When Eve was tempted in the garden, in Genesis 3, satan asked, *"Has God indeed said…"* Satan went on to plant the idea God was withholding from her, and therefore did not have her best interest at heart. Satan caused Eve to question God's true identity as a loving, generous Father. He definitely tempted her to *do* something she was told not to do (eat the fruit). But the inroad to her disobedience—and the consequent fall of mankind—was through challenging Eve's perception of the generous and loving nature of God. Satan tempted Eve by putting into question God's true identity.

Satan used a similar scheme of putting true identity into question when tempting Jesus in the wilderness…

*"Then Jesus was led up by the Spirit into the wilderness to be tempted by the devil. And when He had fasted forty days and forty nights, afterward He was hungry. Now when the tempter came to Him, he said, "**If You are the Son of God**, command that these stones become bread." But He answered and said, "It is written, 'Man shall not live by bread alone, but by every word that proceeds from the mouth of God.'" Then the devil took Him up into the holy city, set Him on the pinnacle of the temple, and said to Him, "**If You are the Son of God**, throw Yourself down. For it is written: 'He shall give His angels charge over you,' and, 'In their hands they shall bear you up, Lest you dash your foot against a stone.'" Jesus said to him, "It is written again, 'You shall not tempt the* LORD

your God.'" Again, the devil took Him up on an exceedingly high mountain, and showed Him all the kingdoms of the world and their glory. And he said to Him, "All these things I will give You if You will fall down and worship me." Then Jesus said to him, "Away with you, Satan! For it is written, 'You shall worship the L*ord your God, and Him only you shall serve.'" Then the devil left Him, and behold, angels came and ministered to Him"* (Matthew 4:1-11).

When Jesus was led out to the wilderness to be tempted by the devil, satan began his temptations with the phrase, "*If* you are the Son of God…." Yes, satan was tempting Jesus to *do* things each time, as he did with Eve. But if you look closely, the temptation was more about satan casting doubts about *who Jesus was*. He was also tempting Jesus to prove Himself. But Jesus understood: *When you know who you are, you have nothing to prove.*

In both cases, with Eve and with Jesus, satan's tactic for mankind's destruction was identity theft! If Eve questioned God's identity as a good and loving Father—thereby questioning her identity as God's daughter—satan had her and all of mankind in the process. If satan could get Jesus to question His identity as God's Son, he had Jesus, and thus our only way of salvation. Satan's scheme worked with Eve because she gave into doubting the goodness of God. Jesus' identity as God's son was secure, and He prevailed.

Our identity is rooted in the answer to this *one* question God asks of each of us in Matthew 16:15, *"But what about **you**? Who do **you** say I am?"*

A.W. Tozer once said, "What comes into our minds when we think about God is the most important thing about us." That could not be any truer. Let me explain.

Today, satan's strategy can often be the same as it was in the garden. It is to get us to question the love of a good God. His plan is to sow seeds of doubt as to God's true nature, His names and His character. Once we fall prey to satan's lies, he causes us to doubt God's love and kind intentions poured out for us, as His sons and daughters. And we lose our true identity in the process.

In other words, once we have a seed of doubt concerning God's goodness—or another aspect of His character—the enemy can ride in on that seed, watering it to maturity. The seed can continue to grow until the truth of who God is becomes altered in our hearts and minds entirely. As God's true identity is whittled away, we also become a shadow of our true selves. And instead of being who we are designed to be, we can find ourselves hiding out in a winepress like Gideon—shrinking back out of fear and unbelief.

LESSONS FROM A FORMER COWARD

"Now the angel of the LORD came and sat under the terebinth at Ophrah, which belonged to Joash the Abiezrite, while his son Gideon was beating out wheat in the winepress **to hide it from the Midianites**. *And the angel of the LORD appeared to him and said to him, "The LORD is with you, O mighty man of valor." And Gideon said to him,* **"Please, my Lord, if the LORD is with us, why then has all this happened to us?** *And where are all his wonderful deeds that our fathers recounted to us, saying, 'Did not the LORD bring us up from Egypt?'* **But now the LORD has forsaken us and given us into the hand of Midian"**

(Judges 6:11-13, ESV).

It's All In A Name

There are some extremely important lessons found in these verses:

1. First, like he did with Eve in the garden, satan plants seeds of doubt as to who God is in our hearts and minds. These seeds of doubt sprout, and if not ripped out by the root, continue to grow until we end up believing the exact opposite of who God is. We can have places in our hearts—even unconsciously—where we believe total lies about God's true nature and character. This, in turn, causes us to believe lies about ourselves. We can even come to believe the exact opposite about ourselves of what is true.

    Notice this progression with Gideon. Gideon doubted God because he hadn't seen God's hand move on behalf of His people in a long time. This morphed into Gideon believing God had forsaken His people, and thus he thought God was "The LORD who forsakes us." This consequently distorted his view of himself. As a result, he was shrinking back from who he was created to be and living in fear as a coward. But the truth is Gideon was designed to be the exact opposite of the man hiding in the winepress. He was designed to be a man of great courage and one valiant in battle.

    This same progression happened to Zachary. During his trip to hell, Zachary was told he was unforgivable. This seed spread. If Zachary was unforgivable, then God's love and sacrifice was not enough for Zachary. God could not save him. And if God could not save him, He was not his Savior. This meant satan had control over him and became more powerful than God in Zach's mind. This, in turn, made Zachary believe his life was lost and subject to the demons terrorizing him. He lived in constant fear as a result. Zachary forgot the truth of

Don't Cheat The Butterfly

who he was. He forgot he was a David, and that he was meant to kill lions and bears. He was designed to be a giant slayer!

2. Another lesson to be learned is that not only does the enemy lie, but our circumstances lie! They neither define *us* nor *God*. Gideon had a distorted view of God because he viewed Him through the lenses of his current circumstances. Things are not always as they appear. That is why what God says in His Word of Himself, and of us as His children, *must trump* our circumstances! Remember, Abraham was told by God he would be a father of a multitude, yet remained childless for what must have seemed an eternity. The enemy will always use our circumstances to lie to us about *who God is* and who He is *on our behalf*.

   I can sure relate to this one. I was looking at my circumstances with regard to Zachary. They were screaming for my attention every day. It appeared God was asleep on the job, and the strategy wasn't working. My circumstances said Zachary was developing a mental disorder. They said he wasn't getting better. This, in turn, said my God either wasn't stronger than the enemy (which I knew wasn't true) or He wasn't moved by our suffering. And my circumstances were all liars! Because the truth is, God is He who weeps with us when we weep and who keeps our tears in His bottle (John 11:33-35 and Psalm 56:8).

3. This one excites me: God used the same strategy with Gideon that He gave me to use with Zachary! I want to share something with you. I have spoken on this on a few occasions. I have used this scripture as an example for the lessons above, along with a couple of others. But I didn't notice *this* particular truth until I wrote this chapter. God literally said to me as I was sitting at my computer, "You're missing something." And I have learned

that when He speaks, I'd better search out the meaning. So I did. I looked back at the verses, and there it was! I had never seen it before.

When the angel of the LORD appeared to Gideon, the first thing out of his mouth was: *"The LORD is with you."* In other words, the angel of the LORD was declaring one of God's many names, an aspect of His nature. He reveals Himself as, "The LORD who is with you." In essence, the angel of the LORD started with telling Gideon the truth of who God is, and correcting his distorted view of God in the process. What is fascinating to note is that a facet of God's character is revealed that is *the exact opposite of the biggest lie* Gideon was presently believing about Him!

The enemy had lied to Gideon, telling him that because he did not see God's intervention on behalf of Israel, God was "the LORD who had forsaken them." And Gideon had bought it—hook, line and sinker.

From Gideon's own mouth, he believed God was *"the LORD who has forsaken us."* But this was a lie from the enemy. The truth was, he needn't be afraid because *"…the LORD your God, He is the One who goes with you. He will not leave you nor forsake you"* (Deuteronomy 31:6). And when God is with and for you, who can be against you (Romans 8:31)?

But that is not all. Because Gideon was believing a lie about God, he also had a distorted view of himself. So after the angel of the LORD tells Gideon the truth about who *God is*, Gideon is then told the truth of who *he is*—a mighty man of valor.

So there you have it. God used the same strategy with Gideon as He did with us to battle an identity theft spirit:

declaring the truth of who God is and the truth of who we are, to bring us out of captivity and fear, and into our true identities.

Be assured, the Lord is our Good Shepherd. He longs to reveal Himself to each of us—in tangible ways—as the opposite of the lies we believe about Him. Not for His sake, to defend Himself, but for our sake. He does so out of His great love for us and to lead us into Truth.

4. The last lesson I will share in this chapter is this: Our true identity—and our destiny—pours forth from God's true identity. Check out what the Lord says to Gideon, the man hiding and cowering in fear, in verse fourteen.

> *"And the* Lord *turned to him and said, 'Go **in this might of yours** and save Israel from the hand of Midian; do not I send you?'"* (Judges 6:14, ESV).

This might of Gideon's? Is God blind? Gideon is in hiding. He appears to be anything but mighty. Gideon is quick to point that out in verse 15…

> *"And he said to him, 'Please, Lord, how can I save Israel? Behold, my clan is the weakest in Manasseh, and I am the least in my father's house'"* (ESV).

Yes, Gideon's circumstances looked grim. It appeared Gideon was correct in his assessment of himself, save one thing. Gideon's true identity was found in God's true identity, not in his challenging situation.

It's All In A Name

Gideon could go in *might* because the Great I AM was sending him, as His ambassador. This is the same when we are in Christ. We are Christ's ambassadors, His *sent ones*, who have the full backing of the Great I AM. We have been given all authority because the One who has commissioned us as His ambassadors has *all* authority.

We are who He says we are. Period. And we *are* because He *is*. Meaning, any good thing or greatness in us comes from the goodness and greatness in Him. What shocks me in the next verse is that it appears God doesn't mind letting us take the credit. Let me explain. Check out how God responds to Gideon in verse 16...

> *"And the* LORD *said to him, 'But I will be with you, and you shall strike the Midianites* **as one man***'" (ESV).*

I have to be honest here. I can totally relate to Gideon's response about being the weakest. The fact is, I said essentially the same thing to God when I found myself constantly facing the enemy's greatest attacks when my husband was unavailable to help. I felt weak and all alone.

But God doesn't see us as we see ourselves. Often when we see ourselves as cowardly, for instance, God calls us "Courageous One!" The truth is, "The LORD who is with you" empowered Gideon to be who God designed him to be—a "mighty man of valor!"

Gideon believed himself a weak man, full of doubt and fear. It would seem from the text that everyone else thought so, too. But it doesn't matter who we, or anyone else for that matter, thinks or says we are. It only matters what God says. And I promise you…His thoughts toward you are so extravagant that if you knew what He says about you, your response would be like Gideon's. Your jaw would drop in shock.

Before it was evident to anyone around him, Gideon's true identity was a "mighty man of valor"—even *while* he was hiding in a winepress. Why? Because God said so. Gideon's identity of being valiant in battle would be birthed from knowing the truth of the almighty, all-powerful aspect of God's nature. Gideon would be victorious because His God was "the LORD who is with you."

What fascinates me in verse 16 is how God puts it. God doesn't say He will *use* Gideon to fight the Midianites *by His (God's) own* power—though this is exactly what happened. God says to Gideon, "And **you** shall strike the Midianites *as one man.*" The truth is that God will do this *through* Gideon by God's *own* power and strength. Yet He is a good Father. Good daddies place their sons on their shoulders so they are able to get the basketball into the hoop, and then they shout, "You did it, son!" Yes, God gives Gideon the credit for what he could never do without Him. What an amazing God we serve!

NOW WHAT?

See the back of this book for a list of scripture references pertaining to the truth of who God is (Who Do You Say I AM: God's Names, Nature and Character) and the truth of who He says we are (Who Do YOU Say I Am: Who I Am in Christ). The Devotional and Bonus Section in the back of the book describes a way to process through them and begin to plant these truths deep in your heart. If you or someone you know is struggling with true identity, this is a great place to start.

But what do you do if someone you love doesn't desire help—or God for that matter? You pray. Ask God how He sees the person. What does God say about them? What is His heart for them? His design for them? Then declare those truths. Pray them. Don't get in the person's face. Don't be "religious" about it. This will only drive them further away.

As Romans 2:4 explains, it is the goodness and kindness of God that leads one to repentance. Speak truth to the person in non-religious language. You can say something like, "When I look at you, I see…" Declare the opposite of their weakness or sin. For instance, if someone is afraid like Zachary was, you could say, "Zachary, when I look at you I see a man of great courage and fearlessness. That is who you are."

Speak these truths when God gives you opportunity. God may even ask you to be silent and only to declare and pray them in the secret place with Him. Be encouraged! There is power in your words, prayers and declarations—regardless of whether the person hears them. The point is to seek God's wisdom and discernment. He will reveal a kingdom strategy for bringing healing and life.

In the next chapter, I will tell you some of the tools we used to discover who Zachary was as an individual. I would like to say a prayer over you before you go on, if you will allow me.

PRAYER

Dear Lord, I ask you to bless this reader—this unique and exquisite one You created in Your image. I ask, Lord, that you would deliver them from a spirit of identity theft. I declare that any lying spirit sowing seeds of doubt or lies into their heart—as to the truth of who You are, and as to the truth of who You created them to be—would be banished from their life. And I declare Your truth over them.

Lord, I ask You to begin to gently pull out the roots of any lies the enemy has sown—directly or indirectly through other people. I ask You to wash and cleanse these places in their heart.

Lord, in place of the lies, I pray You would begin to pour out *Your* names upon them. Manifest Your nature and character in their life—in such personal and tangible ways—that they would begin to see You afresh in truth. I pray You would also show them the truth of who *they* are, as a unique God-breathed individual. Lord, show them the beauty and greatness You have poured into them. We are all created in Your image, and because of that we all carry a measure of Your greatness. It can be no other way.

I pray that the lies of their circumstances, the sins of their past, and the pain and lies of any names stuck to them would be washed away by the power of Your blood that was shed on the cross. I pray a new name would be imprinted on their heart. Lord, launch them on a new journey of discovering You and discovering themselves. And I pray they become "one mighty in valor"!

In Jesus' name, Amen!

CHAPTER FIVE

Identity Quest

But you are a chosen generation, a royal priesthood, a holy nation, His own special people, that you may proclaim the praises of Him who called you out of darkness into His marvelous light.

~Simon Peter, 1 Peter 2:9

THIS GENERATION SEEMS to be searching for identity, whether consciously or unconsciously, like never before. When our crisis first started, Richard and I thought Zachary already had a strong sense of identity. Anyone looking from the outside would have thought so, too. I thought our battle was more about reclaiming his identity from the lies sown during his trip to hell. I wouldn't find out until the writing of this chapter that my assessment was incorrect.

As parents, we aspire to do everything right by our children. As Christian parents, we desire our kids to walk in humility, yet in the strength and fullness of who they were created to be. We also desire our children to grow up knowing God's unconditional love for them. Because of this, Richard and I spoke of God's love and grace constantly. We weren't ones to make our kids feel God was angry with them, and that "they better read their Bible every day or face hellfire and damnation!"

Come to find out, it didn't matter. Zachary felt that, anyway. He explained this was why he kept rededicating his life to God and requesting to be baptized again. He never believed they "took" the first time. And if they did, he felt they were negated because of his sin and disobedience. I was stunned. I actually cried. It was upsetting to find out that a son I had raised believed this, regardless of how I portrayed the extravagantly loving God I know.

It just goes to show that we all have our own walk. We are all on a journey to discover truth and to find God. And we all have an enemy who will use every weapon in his sick, sadistic arsenal to trip us up.

For Zachary, many of the achievements which I had thought came from who he was, actually came from his fear and false perception that he had to *earn* love and acceptance—from God and from those around him. I am so thankful he is not in the same place now. But to think he had these feelings growing up—about himself and about his relationship with God—breaks my heart. Unfortunately, this is not a rare occurrence. We as individuals often attempt to find our identity in many wrong ways and things…

In whose child we are.

What friends we have.

Whose spouse we are.

What possessions we own.

What career we are in.

What talent we possess.

What degree we hold.

What awards we have achieved.

And even what awards and successes our kids have achieved.

Because of this, the answers to these questions can either puff us up with pride or cause us great insecurity, shame and worthlessness. WHY? Because this is a lie from the enemy. He has deceived us into thinking our identity is found in the things of this world—our successes and our failures, and even other people and their opinions.

But this is not our true identity. Our identity is not in who we know, what we do, or what we see in the mirror. Our identity is found in Christ. We hear this all the time in the church, but what does it really mean? And how do we find it?

We are each a reflection of the Lord—a proverbial chip off the old block. We each carry something unique of God's nature—because He is our Creator. A piece of art always reflects a facet of the artist behind it.

God revealed one of His names to Moses in Exodus 3:14, *"And God said to Moses, 'I AM WHO I AM.' And He said, "Thus you shall say to the children of Israel, 'I AM has sent me to you.'"* God is the Great I AM. There is a hidden gem of truth here. I can't know the fullness of who *I am*, nor walk in my God-given calling and destiny, without knowing the *I AM* who created me.

In our home, we raised all three of our sons to know God. We began telling them about the love and greatness of God when they were babies. We read God's Word together daily, and shared what God was doing in our lives continually. Jesus was very much the center and the love of our lives. So when this started with Zachary, he already knew to a large extent who he was. He knew the Bible. He believed in God and had given his life to Jesus as a young boy.

But when we, as God's children, begin to listen to other voices— whether the voice of the world, the media, other people or even demons—God's ever-present voice can be drowned out. Doubt can set in about who God is, opening the door for satan's lies to grow in our hearts. That is why it is imperative that we truly *know* Him.

When I say we must *know* Him, I am not talking about good theology. Yes, it is important to be grounded in the truth of His Word; that is the foundation for all truth. But I am talking about more than *having knowledge of* Him. Remember, Gideon didn't know the true nature of God and therefore didn't know himself. You can be sure Gideon knew *about God*, probably quite a bit. But knowledge is not enough.

When I talk about *knowing* God, I am talking about the Hebrew word **yada**. In Exodus 33:13, Moses says to God, *"Now therefore, I pray, if I have found grace in Your sight, show me now Your way, that I may* **know** *You and that I may find grace in Your sight."*

The Hebrew word used here is *yada,* meaning "to know." But it's not about our intellect. It doesn't mean merely great knowledge about God. It is not about being able to spout scripture. It is not about religion and following all the rules. *Yada* is about intimacy and relationship. It means "to perceive, to know intimately, to understand." *Yada* is the same word used in Genesis 4:1, where it says Adam "knew" Eve and they conceived a child.

God desires that we *yada* Him. He wants us to experience and encounter the different facets of His character, so we *yada* each one, intimately.

> *"But let him who boasts boast in this, that he understands and* **knows** *Me, that I am the* Lord *who practices steadfast love, justice, and righteousness in the earth. For in these things I delight, declares the* Lord*"* (Jeremiah 9:24, ESV).

Gideon felt that he and his people had been abandoned by God, because he didn't *yada* the God who never leaves us nor forsakes us. And out of that misperception of God, he had a misperception of himself.

On the other hand, Simon Bar-Jonah, who was later re-named Peter, experienced and encountered God. He walked with Jesus daily. And out of his *yada* relationship with Jesus, Simon Bar-Jonah not only found himself, but he discovered his destiny in the process.

SOLID AS A ROCK

In Matthew 16:13, Jesus asks a question of His disciples. *"Who do **men** say that I, the Son of Man, am?"* What is Jesus asking here? He is asking, "Who does the world say I am?" He is also asking, "Who do my followers say I am?"

They answer in verse 14 with,

> *"So they said, 'Some say John the Baptist, some Elijah, and others Jeremiah or one of the prophets.'"*

Notice the word "say." Some *say*. We often know the right things to *say*, don't we?

Jesus goes on to ask the disciples in verse 15, *"But who do **you** say that I am?"* This is an individual question, one we are all asked. Whether we realize it or not, we answer this question every day. Our expectation—or lack thereof—of God's interaction in our daily lives answers this question in our hearts, as was seen in Gideon's life.

At this point, Simon Bar-Jonah replies, *"You are the Christ, the Son of the living God."*

The word "Christ" here in the Greek means "Messiah." Simon is declaring Jesus the Messiah, the One they had all been waiting for. Jesus had not yet proclaimed who He was. Simon knew this by revelation.

Simon had ears to hear and eyes to see who Jesus was…because he *hung out with Him*. Simon sat at Jesus' feet and listened to His words. He experienced Jesus' love and power personally, and he witnessed it poured out toward the seemingly *unlovable*. What Simon saw Jesus do for others, he believed and expected for himself as well. He knew by experience that nothing was impossible for God because he watched Jesus do the impossible. But it didn't stop there. Simon then partnered with Jesus to do the same *in* and *through* him.

Simon knew Jesus as Jehovah-Rapha, "the God who heals," because he watched Jesus heal. Simon then made room for God as Healer through *his own hands* when he went out to the streets as Jesus commanded: to heal the sick, cleanse the leper and raise the dead. And the examples go on and on, throughout Simon's life.

In Matthew 16:16, Simon proclaimed Jesus as the Messiah, The Son of God. He saw and believed Jesus for who He is. Let's continue with verse 17.

> *"Jesus answered and said to him, 'Blessed are you, Simon Bar-Jonah, for flesh and blood has not revealed this to you, but My Father who is in heaven.'"*

Now pay attention to what immediately follows in verses 18-19.

*"And I also say to you that **you are Peter**, and **on this rock I will build My church**, and **the gates of Hades shall not prevail against it**. And **I will give you the keys of the kingdom of heaven**, and whatever you bind on earth will be bound in heaven, and whatever you loose on earth will be loosed in heaven."*

What just happened here? Peter found the truth of his own identity through discovering the truth of God's! In this moment, a monumental shift takes place. First, he receives a name change by the Lord. He is no longer "Simon Bar-Jonah." He is no longer simply "Simon the fisherman." Second, Peter learns his calling and God-appointed, original design—God's plan for him from conception. Simon will now forever be remembered as "Peter—the rock, upon which the church is built."

"Your eyes saw my unformed body; all the days ordained for me were written in your book before one of them came to be" (Psalm 139:16, NIV).

What does this concept look like in the daily life of a believer? It is the difference between doing an hour-long devotional that is all about filling yourself with more head knowledge, or running around performing for Him to somehow try to earn His favor, versus sitting at His feet like Mary did in Scripture. At that moment, Mary was not concerned with facts and details, she was simply basking in His presence and drinking Him in.

Yes, read your Bible daily. Yes, engage in activities you feel Him calling you to. But never let these replace those all-important moments when you can just **be** with Him, ponder *who* He is, and allow everything you've learned to make that 18-inch journey from your head to your heart.

Though Jesus gives us a commission to reach the world with His Gospel, we must not forget that He is much more interested in our *being with Him,* like Mary did—as opposed to *doing for Him,* as Martha did. Again, He desires us to "yada" Him—to *know* Him, intimately and experientially, not simply intellectually.

KINGDOM AUTHORITY with Humility

Through *knowing* Jesus in this intimate and experiential way, Peter received a name change and discovered who he was meant to be. But it didn't end there. To top it off, Peter was given a gift—the keys to the kingdom of heaven! It's almost too difficult to believe! Jesus went so far as to tell him that he would have the authority to loose things from heaven into the earthly realm, and to bind things on earth that would then be bound in heaven. This seems too mighty a gift, too lofty an authority. But it was true of Peter. And the amazing thing is…it is true of each one of us who gives our heart and life to Jesus, the one true God.

In John 14:12-14, Jesus said,

> "Most assuredly, I say to you, he who believes in Me, the works that I do he will do also; and greater works than these he will do, because I go to My Father. And whatever you ask in My name, that I will do, that the Father may be glorified in the Son. If you ask anything in My name, I will do it."

Finding our identity in Christ doesn't mean we are insignificant and called to a life of obscurity. In Christ, our true identity is as lofty as Peter's. That's hard for us to believe, but it's scriptural. God designed us each for some measure of greatness. His Word says we are each created in His image. And if that is true, it can be no other way. No one can be a reflection of Almighty God and not have something of great beauty waiting to be revealed to give God glory and to represent Him on the earth.

Todd White says, "If you don't know God's love in an intimate way, you will work to earn it. If you know His love, you'll live to display it." When Jesus asked Peter the question, "Who do you say I am," Jesus knew Peter's answer would determine far more than where Peter would spend eternity. Jesus knew that what Peter believed about Him would determine how Peter would portray Him to the world—as "the rock upon which the church is built." Peter's beliefs of Jesus—His nature and His character—would be the foundation of the Christian faith.

We are to see ourselves in humility, yet in truth. For example, we say things like: "I am just a sinner saved by grace." It is true that we can still sin after being saved. And it is true that we have been saved by grace. But "sinner" is no longer *our identity* when we are in Him. The Bible says that in Him we are now actually saints.

Can you imagine that? I certainly don't feel like a saint. But as I have been trying to convey in this book, truth is not determined by our feelings or the circumstances of our life. Truth is truth, regardless (check out Romans 6 and Ephesians 2:19-22).

We are saints because He says we are, and *only* because of His shed blood. It is not based on our own acts of righteousness. We have no righteousness in us apart from Him. Therefore, we should never walk in pride. That is a given. But remember, when we say things like, "I am just a sinner saved by grace," this is false humility. And false humility is still pride. Why? Because though it has the appearance of humility, in reality it's not. In truth, we think it makes us sound holy. Besides, it is only a partial truth. These partial truths of our identity in Christ cheapen the gospel and the price Jesus paid for us.

Jesus was tortured and died a heinous death—to not only save us, *but* to take back the keys of the kingdom and give them to us. He died that we might have life—and as His sons and daughters, His kings and priests, His friends and His ambassadors. We are not to lay down in the name of *humility* what He died to give us. When He comes for us, He is looking for a return on His investment—a reward for the blood He shed. I, for one, don't wish to offer Him less than the full identity His blood established for me.

His perfect blood changes everything! The veil has been torn. We can now know Him intimately. And as we know Him, sin loses its grip on us. Our love for Him deepens, and serving Him becomes a great joy and fulfillment, not a drudgery birthed out of performance. When we fully know Him and come to understand who we are in Him, we want nothing more than to be who He designed us to be. No worldly pleasure or aspiration will ever come within a fraction of the pure ecstasy of being with Him, and in His presence.

TREASURE HUNT: CLUES TO WHO I AM

Just like Zachary, we all have places in our hearts where we don't see the truth of who we are. In fact, in every place that our hearts believe something of ourselves that doesn't line up with who God says we are, we are believing a lie. This is exactly what the enemy wants. He wants us to believe the opposite of who we are designed to be. Fortunately, God wants us to see ourselves the way He sees us. He wants us to know who we are, in the truth of His plan and design for us. That is why God, in His grace, gives us clues along the way.

God did this for Gideon in Judges 7. In the chapter before, the Lord had told Gideon he was a mighty man of valor who would conquer the Midianites. Yet he was still afraid. Gideon had believed the enemy's lies for so long—that he was the weakest in the land—that Gideon still felt unqualified, unprepared and overwhelmed at the greatness of his calling.

What did God do? Did He chastise him? Reprimand him? Did God change His mind and give Gideon's destiny and calling to another— one stronger and with more faith? No. In God's abundant grace, He sent Gideon down to the enemy's camp, to hear what the enemy had to say about him in secret.

Understand, the enemy will *always* lie to you about who you are. Always. You can only find the truth of who you are designed to be from the Lord. But the enemy is also very well aware of the authority we have been given as God's children. And I believe he also has a *glimpse* of who we are destined to become. That is why he continually hits us with the opposite. But in secret, he shakes in his boots at the thought of you finally coming to know the truth of who you are and were created to become!

Judges 7:9-15 starts out with God speaking to Gideon…

"It happened on the same night that the Lord *said to him, 'Arise, go down against the camp,* **for I have delivered it into your hand**. *But* **if you are afraid to go down**, *go down to the camp with Purah your servant, and* **you shall hear what they say**; *and afterward your hands shall be strengthened to go down against the camp.' Then he went down with Purah his servant to the outpost of the armed men who were in the camp. Now the Midianites and Amalekites, all the people of the East, were lying in the valley as numerous as locusts; and their camels were without number, as the sand by the seashore in multitude. And when Gideon had come, there was a man telling a dream to his companion. He said, 'I have had a dream: To my surprise, a loaf of barley bread tumbled into the camp of Midian; it came to a tent and struck it so that it fell and overturned, and the tent collapsed.' Then his companion answered and said,* **'This is nothing else but the sword of Gideon the son of Joash, a man of Israel! Into his hand God has delivered Midian and the whole camp.'** *And so it was, when Gideon heard the telling of the dream and its interpretation, that he worshiped. He returned to the camp of Israel, and said,*

'Arise, for the LORD *has delivered the camp of Midian into your hand.'"*

We can find many truths of who God says we are as children of God in His Word. I have included several of these in the back of this book. But how can we know who we are uniquely, and what we carry within us as creatively and wonderfully made individuals? How do we help someone else discover this, for that matter? We are each a hidden treasure, waiting to be discovered. And God drops clues along our path of discovery.

Just as with Gideon, one such clue can be found in our trials, our weaknesses—and yes, even our sins. Surprisingly, these often reveal God's intended strength and calling on our lives. In other words, the opposite of these trials, weaknesses and sins is often God's intended design and speaks of our destiny. How? Because of who God is!

God is the God who takes slaves and makes them into princes, as He did with Moses. He is the God who takes the weakest cowards and makes them mighty men of valor, as he did with Gideon. He is the God who takes a barren couple and makes them the parents of a nation, as He did with Abraham and Sarah. He is the God who takes a man like Saul, whose greatest sin was the persecution and murder of Christians, and makes him Paul, the largest contributor of the New Testament, leading countless to life in Christ.

This was God's plan for His people all along. This was in their spiritual DNA when they appeared to be the opposite. If you look at the trials, weaknesses and even the sins of these men, they practically prophesy their calling and destiny. The exact opposite is what God had purposed them to become! How does this truth translate to you and those you love? You can begin to pay attention to your weaknesses and then "come in the opposite spirit" by praying for and intentionally declaring the opposite.

During Zachary's trials, he was in his senior year of high school. He kept saying, "English is my worst subject." But I chose not to grant this declaration power through my agreement. Instead, whenever he spoke this out, I encouraged him to speak and declare the opposite: "English is becoming my best subject!" In the beginning, he did it to pacify me. But as time went on, there was a seed of hope in his heart that dared to believe it could be true.

At the end of the school year, he was invited to the 2012 Graduation Awards. After numerous awards, they announced, "Now the top male English student of the graduating class of 2012, voted on by the entire English Department. Zachary Smeltzer!" You should have seen the look on his face! He couldn't even get up from his chair, and I had to shake him from his stupor. "Go!" I said. Now if that isn't confirmation that this principle is true, I don't know what is!

Besides looking at your weaknesses for clues, you can look at your greatest trials and battles. During his battle, Zachary was blessed to be prayed over and ministered to by two men of faith, Bill Johnson and John Paul Jackson. On separate occasions, each told Zachary he was a "David," yet neither knew him nor that David was his middle name.

As I pondered this, God revealed more and more of how He had been giving Richard and me hints of who Zachary was since the age of two. Believe it or not, the clues began with his dreams. Granted, we named him Zachary David after David in the Bible, and we felt God told us to do so. But you don't necessarily expect that to play out in literal ways.

When King David was a boy, he battled a lion and a bear. This is what prepared him for the giant, Goliath.

"But David said to Saul, 'Your servant used to keep his father's sheep, and when a **lion or a bear** came and took a lamb out of the flock, **I went out after it and struck it**, and delivered the lamb from its mouth; and **when it arose against me, I caught it** by its beard, and **struck and killed it**. Your servant has **killed both lion and bear**; and this uncircumcised Philistine will be like one of them, seeing he has defied the armies of the living God.' Moreover David said, 'The LORD, who delivered me from the paw of the lion and from the paw of the bear, He will deliver me from the hand of this Philistine'" (1 Samuel 17:34-37).

Starting when Zachary was two years old, he began having nightmares of a lion and a bear attacking him—almost nightly. He was terrified to go to sleep because of it. One morning, over a year later, he came into our bedroom early in the morning and woke us up. He was talking excitedly, telling us Jesus had come into his room. He went on to say, "Mommy! Daddy! Wake up! Jesus came in my room last night! Jesus came in my room!" When I questioned him, he continued. "Jesus took His BIG hands and shut the bear and the lion's mouth! He told them to go away and not to come back…and I'M NOT AFRAID ANYMORE!" He never dreamed about a bear or lion again—at least not until the summer of 2011.

Now, as I stated early on, I slept in the room with Zachary for a while during his dark season. The bear dreams had returned with a vengeance. Zachary would be ripped apart each night as he slept, holding my hand to his heart. It was horrific. So when these men said Zachary was a David, my mind immediately went to these nightmares and the ones he had as a young boy. And if Zachary was a David, then he was being trained as a warrior. My husband and I were going to do everything we could to assist in that training.

Job 33:15-18 says,

"In a dream, in a vision of the night, when deep sleep falls upon men, while slumbering on their beds, then He opens the ears of men, and seals their instruction. In order to turn man from his deed, and conceal pride from man, He keeps back his soul from the Pit, and his life from perishing by the sword."

God has been using dreams to speak to mankind since Genesis. If you look through scripture, you can find numerous occasions where God uses dreams to give direction, to warn, to reveal destinies, etc. Are all dreams from the Lord? Are nightmares? No, of course not. But the same principles hold true when we sleep as while we are awake. If the enemy is attacking us, we can take up our spiritual weapons of warfare and fight back. And "The LORD who never leaves us nor forsakes us" will go with us!

It is not okay with God for us to be victims, especially while we sleep. Sleep is designed for peace and rest. I began to train Zachary to call on Jesus in his dreams when being attacked. I also told him to begin to look for a weapon during his nightmares with the bear. He was a David, after all. He was not designed to be the bear's prey; if anything, the bear should be his. Zachary David was designed to be courageous, and I knew God would begin to strengthen this young warrior even in his sleep. I felt that his dreams would reveal where he was on this path, and that one day it would be made manifest during his waking hours.

During this time, we learned another key to knowing who we are designed to become. When these pastors individually prayed for Zachary and told him he was a David, they also added, "What he is going through prophesies to him—or is an indicator of—his calling and destiny." John Paul Jackson said something to the effect that: "The depth, width, length and type of your battle is in proportion to—and reveals—the depth, width, length and type of calling God has on your life." In other words, a fiercer battle can indicate a greater calling. And the type of battle can indicate the type of calling on your life.

C.S Lewis said, *"Hardships often prepare ordinary people for an extraordinary destiny."* This is so true. What I hadn't realized is that the *type* of hardship can also reveal your destiny!

I have found that the best way to understand who you are as a unique, beautifully created individual is to simply ask your Creator. One thing I have done is go before the Lord and *ask Him* who I am. I actually sat down, closed my eyes, and in prayer asked, "Who do You say I am?" I encourage you to do the same. He will begin to show you. I promise.

If you hear something negative, you are not hearing God. Rebuke any voices not of Him in the name of Jesus, and ask again. Ask Him what you "carry into a room with you." What enters a room when you walk into it? Everyone carries something.

Maybe it is hope. Maybe it is peace. Maybe it is creativity. We all carry a unique combination of His likeness and character that God hopes we will learn to deposit in the world around us. We are to be intentional to *be* who we are and to reveal Him wherever we go—simply because we are a reflection of I AM.

True, there are many ways to try to discover who you are apart from God. There are personality tests, DNA tests and the list goes on. But I encourage you, instead, to begin a journey of *yada*—a journey of intimacy with the Great I AM. When you find Him—in truth—you *will* find yourself. And when you find yourself *in Him*, nothing can stop you. Not even the devil himself. But I must warn you, nothing this world has to offer will ever satisfy again.

NOW WHAT?

1. Continue to use the Bonus Section in the back of the book which contains a Devotional, guides for application, and scripture lists. God desires to show you who you are. And that journey begins with *yada*—knowing Him intimately. God longs for intimacy with you. Talk to Him. Begin to look at the scriptures I listed for who God says we are in Him. Meditate on them. Talk to God about them. As an example, God calls us His ambassadors. Ask God what that means and how that looks played out in everyday life.

2. Begin to take an inventory of your greatest weaknesses, your biggest trials and even the sins that seem to repeatedly trip you up. What are the opposites of these things? If your greatest weakness is fear, for example, then the opposite is courage—being a mighty man or woman of valor!

3. Begin to pray and declare the opposite, as I had Zachary do with English. For example, if your struggle is with fear, you can declare: "I am not created for fear! I am a person of great courage! I declare I will become courageous *and* be one to help others walk out of fear and into great courage, also."

4. Take every thought captive. When you hear the negative self-talk, "grab it" and do the above, until your heart begins to dare to believe it.

5. Sit down (as I did), close your eyes in prayer, and envision the Lord asking you the question, "What about you? Who do you say that I am?" Tell Him who you believe Him to be, from your heart. Or tell Him what facet of His nature and character you are believing Him to be for you in this season.

6. While still in that quiet place with Him in prayer, ask Him the same question about yourself. "Who do You say *I* am, Lord?"

He will begin to show you. I promise. If you hear something negative, you are not hearing God. Rebuke any voices not of Him in the name of Jesus, and ask again. This may take some time. Sometimes we have such lies in our hearts that we can't hear through all the muck. Keep asking. He will begin to show you who you are.

7. Ask Him what you "carry into a room with you." What beautiful combination of the facets of His nature do you carry within you? What enters a room when you walk into it? Ask God to help you to be intentional to deposit this "as you go."

PRAYER

Lord, I thank You that I have been made in Your image, a beautifully unique and God-designed individual. Lord, I give you my weaknesses and ask You to make them my strengths. I give You my trials and trust You to give me beauty for ashes.

I bring my sins to the foot of the cross. (Take time to be specific.) I ask You to forgive me and to wash me white as snow by Your shed blood for me. I ask You to take my sins, now placed under the cross, and that one day You would give me the blessing of helping others walk in freedom from those same sins of my past.

I pray I would begin to see who You are in truth. I pray I would begin to *yada*—to truly know and experience in intimate ways—the different facets of your nature and character. I pray they would manifest in my life in tangible ways I can recognize. And I pray that out of knowing You more fully, I would begin to see the truth of who I am.

I pray that any identity theft spirit attacking me, or the members of my family, would be defeated in our lives. I pray not one would succumb to the lies of the enemy. And I pray the enemy of my soul will no longer wield power to lie to me and keep me from who You created me to be. Show me the truth of who I am, based on what *You* say of me. I ask You to teach me how to see and discern who others are, uniquely, in Your eyes. Teach me ways to convey the truths you show me of others, so they will receive Your truth in their hearts.

Lord, I ask You, "Who do You say I am?" Show me who I am—according to Your Word, and also according to my own unique design. Show me what I carry with me when I walk into a room. And help me to walk into my God-ordained destiny and purpose.

You are the Great I AM! I desire to *yada* You. Continue to train me and to reveal more of Yourself to me, even as I sleep. In Jesus' mighty and all-powerful name! Amen!

CHAPTER SIX

Don't Cheat the Butterfly

What the caterpillar calls the end of the world, the master calls a butterfly.

~Richard Bach

EVERY WAR HAS a beginning, a middle and an end—but ours seemed to be on a perpetual loop. In November of 2011, three months into the battle, Zachary decided it was time to learn to stand alone. Or lie down to sleep alone, anyway. I had moved back into our master bedroom, but I continued carrying the burden of our son through the night, only now from the other side of the house. I had not yet learned to lay this burden down at Jesus' more-than-capable feet.

Zachary was making baby steps toward recovery, and we tried to celebrate each one. He was gradually learning to cope. But merely coping was not an option in my book. I was not fighting for my son to barely exist; I was fighting for victory. We continued using the strategy God gave me, daily. Day, after day, after day. Zachary's hour-long showers had become a ritual after returning from school. He would crank up the worship music, stand under the hot water, and try to find a reprieve for his soul.

We had enlisted some mighty prayer warriors from the start, and they continued ever-faithful—month after month in our never-ending war. It seemed I would send out a praise report one day, only to send out a desperate plea for help the next.

We were somewhere in 2012 now. When you are walking through darkness, the days all look the same. On one such day, Zachary came to me in his all-too-familiar terrorized state. He grabbed my hand, unable to speak. "I thought we were past this," I thought to myself. By this point, Zachary was usually able to verbalize he was under attack. I began, "Who is God, Zachary?…Tell me who you are."

Zachary and I had grown quite attached by now. We could read each other fairly well. Before this year, Zachary had always been a "Daddy's boy." Now, nearing manhood, he was quite attached to my apron strings. A mother always wants the love of her son, but she doesn't want him dependent on her when it is nearing his time to leave the nest.

Zachary had always been college bound. Now he could barely make it through a day of high school without calling me from his car, crying, asking me to pick him up. We were nearing his 43 absences and tardies for his senior year, by then. How would that fare for his finals come June? How could he ever leave our home like this? This all ran through my mind—a swirling jumbled mess of emotions, threatening to take me under.

What happened next is forever etched in my memory. I was about to behold the most courageous act I have ever witnessed with my own eyes—and to catch a glimpse of the mighty warrior my son would become.

When the worst of it had passed and Zachary had some presence of mind again, he saw the fear in my eyes. Zachary grabbed my hand again—this time reassuring *me*—and said, "It's okay, Mom. Don't worry. I have asked God not to remove this *one day before* He accomplishes all He wants to in me, and until there is nothing in me that would ever be satisfied to go back to who I was before."

WHAT? I was astounded! How was he able to say this in the midst of his atrocious battlefield trauma, and after living this way—daily—for *months*? I certainly wasn't. I wanted this *over*! What was he thinking? *My* heart was screaming, "Enough already!" But *his* heart was miraculously at rest—with torment.

What soldier, in an endless bloody war, asks for the battle to rage on—so he can be perfected? This was not about being perfect. It was no longer about performance. It was about submitting to what God was accomplishing in him. Zachary somehow knew, even in the mental state he was in, that God was producing a *good* work in him. He didn't want to short-circuit it, no matter how gruesome the heat of battle. In the eyes of God, I knew this war hero had just been pinned with the Medal of Honor, though the war was not yet over.

A MESSAGE AT DAWN

Around this time, Andrea, a dear friend of mine, woke up from a sound sleep and heard the sentence, "Don't cheat the butterfly." She shared it with our group of friends, and we began to ponder its meaning and do some research.

We learned that the flight muscles of a butterfly are developed in the struggle to break free of the cocoon. It is actually the process of breaking out of the cocoon that affords the butterfly strength and the ability to fly. To be broken free of the cocoon prematurely causes the butterfly to die. Therefore, the process of living in the darkness of the cocoon, and the subsequent struggle to emerge from it, plays a huge part in the butterfly's destiny.

> *"Perhaps the butterfly is proof that you can go through a great deal of darkness, yet become something beautiful."* ~Unknown

I knew what God was saying, though it was hard to accept. He was telling me not to despise the process—but to actually embrace it. It took my teenage son to teach me, however, that sometimes in fighting the enemy, you can cross over the line and fight God Himself. Why? Because sometimes God is producing far greater fruit and victory in the wait—in the struggle to break free of the cocoon—than in the final act of emerging. Zachary was willing to submit to the process, in full faith that he would come out metamorphosed on the other side.

> *"Count it all joy, my brothers, when you meet trials of various kinds, for you know that the testing of your faith produces steadfastness. And let steadfastness have its full effect, that you may be perfect and complete, lacking in nothing"* (James 1:2-4, ESV).

The word "steadfastness" is a Greek word meaning "enduring, patience, steadfastness, perseverance and constancy." Having steadfastness in trials is pressing through our pain. We are a society that avoids pain at all costs. But Jesus, for the joy set before Him, endured the cross (Hebrews 12:2). He could have come down. He could have alleviated His own pain. He had the power to *cheat the butterfly*. But He knew the victory that would result if He stayed the course. So He endured.

You can find this principle throughout scripture, in the lives of individuals like Joseph (as I will explain later in this chapter). You can also see it played out with the nation of Israel.

*"**Little by little** I will drive them out before you, **until you have increased enough** to take possession of the land"* (Exodus 23:30, NIV).

*"You shall not be terrified of them; for the L*ORD *your God, the great and awesome God, is among you. And the L*ORD *your God will drive out those nations before you **little by little; you will be unable to destroy them at once**, lest the beasts of the field become too numerous for you. But the L*ORD *your God will deliver them over to you, and will inflict defeat upon them until they are destroyed"* (Deuteronomy 7:21-23).

*"Therefore **the L*ORD **will wait, that He may be gracious to you;** *And therefore He will be exalted, that He may have mercy on you. For the L*ORD *is a God of justice;* **Blessed are all those who wait for Him"** (Isaiah 30:18).

When you value the process, you begin to see things differently. Your destiny isn't simply in the distant future, but is also found in each stage of your development. As my friends and I continued to research this, we found that the DNA of a butterfly already exists in the caterpillar!

And it is the same with us! The spiritual DNA of who God created us to be resides in us before we walk in any of it. It resides in us while still cramped in a dark cocoon. It is the process—the trials and the struggle to emerge—that births in us the strength and ability to spread our wings and fly.

Let me be clear. I am not telling you to embrace an attack from the enemy, or to put up with it for what it will produce in you. As you can see, we fought with everything in us. I am simply saying God will *never* waste our trials. He will take what the enemy means for evil and He *will* work it for good. He will produce something profound from it if we allow patience to have its perfect work.

This principle holds true for our many seasons in life, not just when under heavy assault. In this culture and time in history, we often want to get on to the next thing—either out of sheer boredom and our thirst for adventure, or as a means of escape. The truth is, sometimes we are running from our past, our current situation, and even ourselves.

It seems we either strive for the next stage or lament the previous one, instead of choosing to bloom where we are planted. We talk about "when I finish college," "when I land that job," or "when I get married." Then it becomes "when we have children," "when our kids graduate and move out," and "when we retire."

On and on it goes until we have wished away our lives. We are always looking to the distant or not-so-distant future where our peace and happiness reside. We make plans—and even knock down closed doors to get there—hoping it resembles what we have envisioned once we have *arrived*. But as my dad always said, "No matter where you go, there you are."

The truth is, sometimes God is producing the most fruit in us when our cars are stuck in the parking lot—when we are somewhere between point A and point B. It is the steadfastness in the waiting that prepares us for what is around the next corner. The transition stages are often the most painful, but they also give us wings.

My one word of caution would be: while embracing the painful process, do not allow the pain to become your identity. Take sickness, for example. Yes, God will always produce beauty from our seasons of illness, but we are *not* our diseases. Nor are we our trials. When we identify with our pain—and especially when it serves us somehow, as in giving us attention we enjoy—then we have gone past embracing what God is doing in the wait, and we are now embracing what the enemy is doing. We must be mindful of the difference.

THE PRICE OF VICTORY

One day at my women's group, while I was sharing about my struggles, a dear friend grabbed my shoulders, looked me square in the eyes and said, "Oh honey, did you really think it would cost you nothing?" She was talking about the cost for the things I had cried out to God for—the cost of a calling, a message, a voice, and something on this earth that would have some eternal value.

My closest friends know that I have always asked God that I might be "the one who touches Your heart." Oftentimes, the things our hearts desire in the Lord cost us something. There were times during this dark season with Zachary when I felt it wasn't worth it. I didn't want the cost. I didn't want the pain. I just wanted my son back.

Maybe you are in a dark place, too. Maybe you are reading this and saying as I did, "Whatever this may be producing in me, it's not worth it." Well, I would like to propose a question. What if it is?

What if this life is only training? What if the meaning of life on earth is all about eternity, instead of the here and now? What if the pain we endure in this life is over in a blink of an eye, and God will soon wipe away every tear? What if we gain authority through our hardships that equips us for the rest of our earthly lives and then on into eternity, where God says we will rule and reign with Him?

> *"For if we died with Him, we shall also live with Him.*
> *If we endure, we shall also reign with Him"* (2 Timothy 2:11-12a).

I think of the old movie "Karate Kid." Wax on, wax off. Day after day, Daniel-san was forced to do menial tasks by his sensei, Mr. Miyagi. Daniel just wanted to get on with it and learn how to fight! He thought waxing the car and painting the fence were a waste of his time, not to mention a backache. But the truth was he was being prepared to be a warrior. What if he had walked away? It would have made for a really boring movie. But far more than that…Daniel wouldn't have become a conqueror!

I am not speaking of championships and receiving awards and trophies. I am speaking of who he became. He became who he was always meant to be. Someone of greatness. More than a survivor, he was a victor.

When we desire to make an impact on this earth—there is a cost. If we aspire to more than simply *making it to heaven by the skin of our teeth*—there is a cost. Every Bible hero we admire paid a great price. King David determined never to give to the Lord that which cost him nothing.

> *"Then King David said to Ornan, 'No, but I will surely buy it for the full price, for I will not take what is yours for the* Lord, *nor offer burnt offerings with that which costs me nothing'"* (1 Chronicles 21:24).

Is it worth the sacrifice? Is it worth the cost? There was a time I told the Lord to "pick someone else. This is too hard!" I am so thankful He turned a deaf ear.

DISCOVERING GOD'S GOODNESS

A dear and wise friend once told me, "Kristen, *all* things work together for good for those who love the Lord." Yes, he was simply quoting Romans 8:28. But at 86 years of age, Harald Bredesen spoke from experience—from a *yada* place of knowing God—not from his head knowledge. He could look back over the course of nearly nine decades of life and say, "Yes. With God, they *all* certainly do! Not just the simple things, but the impossible ones as well."

We all have times and circumstances in life that test this simple truth. There were so many days I looked at Zachary and struggled with the question, "Lord, how can You bring good from *this*? How can you bring beauty from these ashes?"

So how *can* God take something tragic in our lives and bring good from it? The answer isn't found so much in the "how," but in the "Who." The answer is found in *who* God is. It is found in His character. It is found in the essence of His presence, in the fragrance of His being. He is the Great Restorer. He is the One Who Redeems All Things. The answer is found in His love toward us. It is found in a love so encompassing—so extravagant—we have not the mind to comprehend it.

It is *who* God is that empowers the promise. To say we are without hope in a situation is to say God is not God. It is to say He is impotent in power. It is to say He is not loving, kind or good.

All through Scripture, you can find examples of God's people feeling abandoned by Him. Yet as with Gideon, God always had a plan—a beautiful tapestry of His bountiful love—waiting to be revealed in the end.

Another great example is the story of Joseph, found in Genesis. While Joseph was yet a boy, God told him in a dream he would become great and the leader of his people. Out of jealousy, his own brothers plotted to kill him, but decided to sell him into slavery instead. Joseph was taken in shackles to Egypt, and was later wrongly accused and sent to prison. All seemed lost. At this point, the dream God gave him seemed more like a cruel joke. Yet God had a plan.

Instead of falling into self-pity or allowing himself to be a victim, Joseph determined to bloom where he was planted. Eventually Joseph was released from prison and placed second in command of Egypt. When a famine spread throughout the region, Joseph's brothers left their country in search of food and ended up coming for help before their own brother, not even recognizing him because so many years had passed. Joseph revealed his identity, forgave his brothers and provided for them.

If Joseph hadn't experienced his earlier hardships—if he had found a way of escape, instead of embracing the arduous and lengthy process—he, his family *and his country* would have perished. Instead, an entire nation was preserved through the very circumstances that appeared to display the cruelty or absence of God.

As for me, I knew God did not *do* any of this to Zach. I was upset because He wasn't stopping it in my way and according to my timetable. And this was wrong. It was the response of my soul. Trusting that God is good—in the midst of our trials—is a stance of war and a powerful weapon. It is a faith that moves mountains.

I had to come to a place of trusting God's goodness in the midst of my offense, like Peter, and in the midst of the long wait. God's goodness is truth. His goodness was present before Zachary's healing. His goodness was present during his trial. And His goodness would be present even if Zachary showed no signs of improvement this side of heaven. God is good because that's who He is. He is perfect love, and in Him is no evil.

Trusting in God's goodness means not needing to have all the answers. It is loving Him in spite of my unanswered questions. It is knowing I have no need to jump through hoops for His attention. It is understanding that I have no need to beg, barter or twist God's arm to hear my prayers. It is knowing I have His ear, because He is the God who loves and hears me.

One day it *will* have all been worth it! God *will* wipe every tear from our eyes and give us joy for our darkest hours. Why? Because He is the God who keeps His promises. Because He is the God who gives good gifts to His children. Because He is the God who gives us beauty for our ashes. Because He is the God of justice who redeems and restores all things. Why? Because He loves us. Because it is *who* He is!

"Now to Him who is able to do immeasurably more than all we ask or imagine" (Ephesians 3:20).

A HERO'S STRIDE

In our darkest hours, God poses the question, "Do you, too, wish to walk away?" And we have the opportunity to say unequivocally, "No! Where else would I go? Only You have the words of life." The only way to walk through the valley of the shadow of death is to keep on walking, one step at a time. But there are ways to make that walk a little more bearable, and a lot more fruitful. One is to realize it is not all about you.

When going through something difficult, it is easy to become so self-absorbed that you don't see the pain in others. But it is a profound truth that you can unleash healing in your own life as you give to others out of your place of deepest need. When you need a miracle, what more beautiful a sacrifice than to be a miracle for someone else? Zachary understood this principle. In response, Zachary and his twin brother, Jacob, asked to go on a mission trip to Europe with our missionary friend who baptized Zachary when this all first started.

Revelation 19:10 says, *"The testimony of Jesus is the spirit of prophecy."* I do not propose to know the full measure of this verse's meaning. But I do know that God uses the testimony of what Jesus is doing in and for us, to bring hope to others. I can look at someone's life and say, "If God can do that for you, He can do it for me. If you can find victory over your enemy, I certainly can, too." The testimony you are earning through your trials can be a prophecy for someone else.

Another way to walk through your valley is to dance instead—even when you feel like it's enough just to crawl. David danced before the Lord. And he didn't care who watched and how ridiculous he looked, either.

2 Samuel 6:14 says, *"Then David danced before the Lord with all his might; and David was wearing a linen ephod."* David understood the meaning of a sacrifice of praise. *"Therefore by Him let us continually offer the **sacrifice of praise to God**, that is, the fruit of our lips, giving thanks to His name"* (Hebrews 13:15).

A sacrifice of praise is not praising God for the victory once your ship has come in. If I could have seen into the future during Zachary's attacks, and known what it would produce, I would have easily danced for joy. But a sacrifice of praise is just that—a sacrifice. It is being able to dance before Him in thanksgiving *before* you get your miracle, and even if you never do.

While in the midst of our darkness, Richard received this revelation. He felt he needed to take Zachary into the woods with his Bible: to read the Psalms, to sing God's praises and to dance before the Lord—before we saw God's miraculous hand in our circumstances. So he did just that.

How could Richard do this? How can *you* do this? Again, because of *who God is*. It is a weapon of warfare to rejoice in the Lord, in full confidence of what God will produce from your darkness, and in the face of insurmountable evidence to the contrary. Richard and Zachary went into a wooded area across the street from our house and offered up to God a beautiful sacrifice. It was shortly thereafter that things would shift. In the woods they gave God praise. And it would be in those same woods that Zachary would soon find his victory.

SILENCE IS GOLDEN

One of the best ways to survive chaos and hardship is to get silent and listen for His voice. We are created spirit, soul and body—and in that order. Yet we are often ruled by our flesh and our soul (mind, will and emotions).

During this season, especially, God began to teach me to tap into His Spirit by listening with my spirit—instead of being ruled by what my eyes *saw* and what my emotions *felt*. Worship helps one do this. I would put on some worship music, get quiet and pray, "God, what are *You* saying about this situation?" It is a discipline—and can be difficult in the beginning—but it's so worth the exercise. Your spiritual hearing muscles will be strengthened, and it will be easier each time.

To hear *His* voice, we have to tune out the others. If we can tap into His peace and rest, all the better. Graham Cooke says, "To rest in God's power when your own weaknesses seem to be screaming at you? That's grace! To be confident in who God is for you when you feel overwhelmed by odds against you? That's peace! To stand alone against massive intimidation? That's trust! To know beyond any shadow of a doubt that God is bigger, and therefore you cannot lose? That's the faith that moves mountains!"

While going through this season with Zachary, there were so many voices screaming at me and stealing my peace. Some were the voice of the enemy, some other people, some the media, and some my own emotions. It is wise to be discerning of whose voice you're tuned into. One way to know is: If you are not at rest and peace, you're tuned into the wrong voice. And you certainly are not tuned into God's.

Now, when I receive bad news or have an uneasy feeling about something, I pause and ask…"Is there truth to this, God? Should I pray? Is everything okay? What are You saying about this?" Often, the anxiety I am feeling is completely released because I can sense His peace and know there is no truth to my anxious concerns. At other times, He may ask me to pray until I feel a peace and a shift in my heart. This is a powerful tool to release anxiety and control, and to place trust back in God's hands where it belongs.

So how do you hear His voice? Over the years of walking with God, I have learned to recognize His voice. I don't hear Him audibly. It is a "still small voice," as some call it. It often sounds like my own thoughts. But when you are intentional to listen and hear Him, and even when you are minding your own business, you will notice the difference. For one thing, what He says usually sounds nothing like you. His voice does not always agree with yours, either. In fact, many times it won't.

Remember in the beginning when I shared that God often speaks questions or thought-provoking statements into my head that take me on a journey of some sort? Before all this began with Zachary, I struggled to get quiet before God. So He had a habit of speaking to me when I was showering or blow-drying my hair. I joke that it is because I'm Italian, and I talk too much. But these were God's best opportunities to speak to me.

A few months before this all started with Zachary, I was blow-drying my hair—minding my own business—when God interrupted my thoughts with one of those statements. He said, "You think you're a better parent than I am." It wasn't an accusation. He was getting me to think. I immediately turned off the blow-dryer.

"What?" I replied, bewildered. "I don't believe I am a better parent than You, Lord. In fact, I often feel quite inadequate. Why would You say that?" He then, very kindly but firmly, showed me my heart.

At the time, He was saying something particular that pertained to my current circumstances. But a couple months into this situation with Zachary, God gently said it again. I defended myself with all the ways I felt like a failure as a mother—my mistakes, shortcomings and inadequacies.

"How could You say I think I am a better parent than You, Lord?" Again, He kindly replied by showing me the thoughts of my heart. "Your heart says, 'If I was God, I would take down the enemy! If I was God, I would heal Zachary. If I was God, I would use my power to do something!'"

And there it was. It was so true. My heart was exposed. I hadn't even realized it, but I thought I was a better parent than God, after all. God gently pointed me to truth. I learned that any place where my heart believes I have more love, compassion or mercy than God, I have elevated myself above Him and am believing a lie. And any place where I have placed limits on His love and power, I have humanized Him and reduced Him to what my mind can comprehend.

In the places of my heart where I believed, albeit subconsciously, that I loved my sons more than God did, in the places I positioned myself to twist God's arm on Zachary's behalf, I was putting my love on a greater plane than the Lord's. Basically, I was putting myself on the cross and saying my love and sacrifice was greater. I was deeply grieved at this realization and repented. Again, my repentance was only met with His kindness and gentleness.

Through hearing His voice speak only one sentence, God not only revealed my heart, but He wooed me and restored my trust in His goodness, as well. Getting quiet to hear His voice is a lifeline that keeps us secure on His path and develops intimacy with the Lover of our Souls.

NOW WHAT?

1. Ask yourself, "Am I trying to cheat the butterfly in my life? How can I embrace the process and what God is accomplishing through it, while not coming into agreement with what the enemy is doing? Am I mindful of the difference between embracing the process and not allowing my pain and trial to become my identity? Is there a place in me that enjoys the 'benefits' of what I am going through?"
2. If you feel the need to repent in regard to your answers to any of the above questions, do so. He is so gracious and kind. Have a conversation with Him, and ask Him what it looks like in your personal life to keep yourself from "cheating the butterfly," while still contending for healing and deliverance.
3. Do you desire to make your mark on this earth? Have you been willing to count the cost? Could some of your struggles simply be God training you for what you have asked Him for? Are you trying to short-circuit your training? Ask Him for wisdom to understand what is actually the enemy at work in your life versus what is simply God allowing you to be buffeted and trained for your destiny.

4. Are you trusting in God's goodness for you, personally? Are you anticipating Him working everything for your good? Or is there doubt in your heart? Do some business with God, and hash it out with Him. He desires to renew your hope and give you a glimpse of His extravagant love for you. He wants you to have the confidence of His plans, already set in motion on your behalf.

5. He is asking you, "Do you wish to walk away?" He is waiting for your resolute, "No! Only You have the words of life." Think about ways you can have a *hero's stride* in the waiting. Can you be intentional to be outwardly focused and be the miracle for someone else? Can you offer up to God a sacrifice of praise? Can your testimony be a prophecy—an encouragement—for someone else?

6. Intentionally take time to get silent before Him. Train yourself to listen for His still small voice. He longs to speak to you and reveal Himself to you in unique and tangible ways.

7. Are there places in your heart where "you think you are a better parent than Him?" Spend some time repenting and offering Him up your trust again. He is so worthy of your complete trust.

PRAYER

Dear Lord, I don't want to cheat the butterfly. I want to emerge from my dark places with wings to fly. Help me to embrace the process while still contending for Your will in my circumstances. Please forgive me for any place in my life where I have identified with my pain and trials, because they give me attention or benefit me in some way. I ask

Your forgiveness. I desire to walk into the fullness of who You have created me to be.

Lord, I struggle to believe You have greatness for me and my life. I choose, in faith, to believe Your Word. In the places I have been afraid of counting the cost, or I have walked away from my calling because it seems too daunting, I repent. I ask You to equip me, strengthen me and give me the steadfastness to endure until the end.

Lord, I long to know You intimately and experientially—to *yada* You—and to hear Your voice. Teach me to silence the other voices in my head so I can hear You more clearly. I invite You to speak to me and take me on a journey with the words You speak to my heart.

Please forgive me for the places I have thought I am a better parent than You, or a better friend than You. Forgive me for elevating myself and believing I somehow have more knowledge, love and compassion than You. I declare You to be a *good*, *good* Father. I give my full trust to You now, in faith. You are worthy of my trust. In Jesus' name, Amen.

PART TWO

Spoils of War

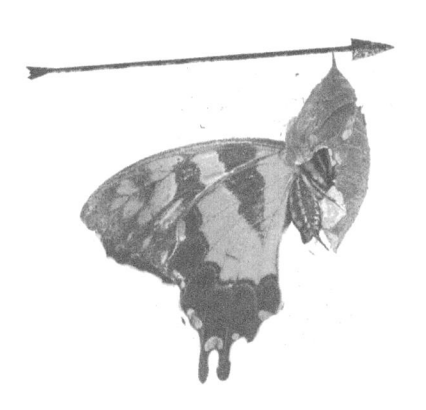

To the victor belong the spoils.

~William L. Marcy

CHAPTER SEVEN

Tilted Scales

For the LORD *loves justice, and does not forsake His saints.*

~King David, Psalm 37:28

After months of struggle, we finally turned a corner, and I sensed Zachary was improving. I'm not sure what finally tipped the scale, but little by little he learned to fight the enemy without me. Sadly, he still seemed to be living in survival mode, and I longed for the day when the light and joy would return to his eyes.

He graduated from high school on June 8, 2012, and in spite of his 43 absences and tardies for his senior year, he received a 4.0 and graduated with high honors. This was just one testimony of God's faithfulness. Instead of college, he decided to apply to a non-accredited ministry school in Redding, California. He was accepted, and I felt a burden lift off his shoulders. One lifted off mine, as well. Leaving home would be a big step, and knowing he would be surrounded by other believers pursuing God gave me some peace.

Even though the intensity of his battle had decreased over the last couple months, it had been a long, traumatic year. We were the walking wounded, arm in arm, slowly making our way off the battlefield. I so desired Zachary to be able to walk this alone when he left our home come September, and I still couldn't imagine him a couple of states away without us by his side. So I continued to pray and ask God to give me faith and an assurance He would take care of my son when he spread his wings to fly.

"HEAR YE! HEAR YE!"

> *"'Present your case,' says the* Lord. *'Set forth your arguments,' says Jacob's King"* (Isaiah 41:21, NIV).

Most know the old phrase the bailiff calls out when announcing the judge's arrival in the courtroom. I particularly like the verbiage used by the Florida State Supreme Court: "All rise. Hear ye, hear ye! The Supreme Court is now in session. All those who have cause to plea, draw near and you shall be heard."

All through Scripture you can find verses about God's love of justice. You can find scriptures about His courts and bringing your case before Him. He is the God who vindicates and restores. He is the God who executes righteousness on the earth. He is the God who requires thieves to make restitution.

I shared in an earlier chapter that Zachary was blessed to be prayed over by two men of faith—Bill Johnson and John Paul Jackson. They explained that the depth, width, length and type of our battles are in proportion to and reveal to us the depth, width, length and type of calling God has on our lives. In other words, the greater the calling, the greater the battle. And the type of battle indicates the type of calling on our lives.

I would go on to learn that the depth, width, length and type of battle you have suffered is also indicative of what is owed you in compensation before our Just Judge. God began to show me, through His Word, that He loves when His children go before Him and ask Him for pure things to compensate them for their damages!

What are "pure things"? Certainly not judgment on others, or for evil to befall those who have wronged us. I am *not* speaking about asking God to rain down judgment on man. We are called to forgive man. For our part, when we wrong another we can find forgiveness through repentance, but God often asks us to go a step further and make restitution. Restitution can be an integral part of the healing process on both sides of the equation.

But I'm not referring here to wrongs done by or toward another human. I am speaking about what we have a "legal right" to ask God for, in regard to the havoc the *enemy* has wreaked in our lives.

We began to pray this way for Zachary, going before the Lord and presenting our case. Let me be clear: God doesn't owe us anything, because He doesn't wrong us. The case we presented was *not* against God, but against the enemy of our souls. He is the thief who comes *"to steal, to kill and to destroy"* (see John 10:10).

Sometimes the enemy attacks us when we are innocent, as in the case of Job in Scripture. God was just in blessing Job with all that He did, because of all Job had lost. God allowed the enemy to sift him and steal from him, knowing all along He would be just in restoring *to him* double for what the enemy took *from him*. And Job's latter years were greater than his former, as a result.

> *"And the LORD restored Job's losses when he prayed for his friends. Indeed the LORD gave Job twice as much as he had before.... Now the LORD blessed the latter days of Job more than his beginning; for*

he had fourteen thousand sheep, six thousand camels, one thousand yoke of oxen, and one thousand female donkeys" (Job 42:10, 12).

You may recall the enemy also petitioned to sift Peter like wheat. Jesus didn't tell Peter that He denied satan's request. He merely told Peter that He had prayed for him to come through victorious. Not too comforting. Yet, the sifting allowed God—as the Just Judge—to bless Peter abundantly in the end!

"And the Lord said, 'Simon, Simon! Indeed, Satan has asked for you, that he may sift you as wheat. But I have prayed for you, that your faith should not fail; and when you have returned to Me, strengthen your brethren'" (Luke 22:31-32).

The sifting was part of Peter's cocoon process. And he was transformed as a result. When he came out the other side, he carried great authority in the Spirit and became the rock upon which the church was built.

Yes, sometimes we are attacked when innocent. Other times we can bring attacks on ourselves, by opening a door through our own sin and unwise choices. When we sin, the enemy has a "legal right" to come in. In other words, our case against him is no longer considered "illegal or forced entry."

This is what happened with Zachary. He dabbled with things that allowed the enemy entrance. But one of the amazing attributes of God is that when we repent of the sins that give the enemy legal access—as Zachary had that first night in 2011—our record is expunged!

Understand, our sins and unwise choices carry repercussions that can impact us for years to come. But even these don't disqualify us from God's love and blessings. Yes, they may make our path more difficult. But remember that God knows all of our choices in advance. And

He is so merciful that when we repent, He blesses us *regardless* of the mistakes we made.

That's exactly what happened with Zachary. Did God want Zach to smoke pot and go through what he did? Of course not. But obviously God used it to bring about something beautiful. The key, again, is true repentance.

When we repent, God expunges our heavenly record. This expungement thoroughly wipes the slate clean with His blood so that—in the heavenly realm—there is no remaining evidence of a crime (sin) ever being committed! God even promises *He* won't remember these sins—ever again (Isaiah 43:25)! Yes, we may still see some consequences in the natural realm, but God is powerful enough to overcome those obstacles.

"Have mercy upon me, O God,
According to Your lovingkindness;
According to the multitude of Your tender mercies,
Blot out my transgressions.
Wash me thoroughly from my iniquity,
And cleanse me from my sin.

For I acknowledge my transgressions,
And my sin is always before me.
Against You, You only, have I sinned,
And done this evil in Your sight—
That You may be found just when You speak,
And blameless when You judge"

(Psalm 51:1-4).

For God to judge in our favor as our Just Judge, we must be found innocent. For this to occur, our sin has to be covered under His blood, through our repentance. Once we repent and receive forgiveness, our sin is stricken from the record, so to speak, and God can render a verdict against the enemy in our favor.

Knowing this, the first thing we must do when going before God in prayer, as our Just Judge, is to lay our hearts bare before Him. Invite Him to search your heart for any legal ground the enemy may have against you.

> *"Search me [thoroughly], O God, and know my heart; Test me and know my anxious thoughts; and see if there is any wicked or hurtful way in me, and lead me in the everlasting way"* (Psalm 139:23-24, AMP).

God is faithful. He will bring something to mind—whether it be a word, a picture or a memory—if there is something to be addressed. Keep in mind, God will not parade in front of you something you already repented of. Only the enemy does that. Scripture says it is God's *kindness* that leads us to repentance (Romans 2:4). God will only show you, in love, what has not been thoroughly dealt with.

If He reveals something, work it through with Him. He loves our repentance, and it frees His hand to bless us. Once sin is dealt with and cleansed under His blood, you can approach Him as your Just Judge and request Jesus to plead your case on your behalf. Then you can pray and ask God for what you would like in return for the judgment against your adversary, the devil. God, in His justice, can then issue "court-appointed restitution."

> *"Do not rejoice over me, my enemy; When I fall, I will arise; When I sit in darkness, The* LORD *will be a light to me. I will bear the*

indignation of the LORD, *because I have sinned against Him,* **until He pleads my case and executes justice for me**. *He will bring me forth to the light;* **I will see His righteousness**. *Then she who is my enemy will see, and shame will cover her who said to me, 'Where is the* LORD *your God?' My eyes will see her; Now she will be trampled down like mud in the streets"* (Micah 7:8-10).

For us, we asked God that Zachary would one day be blessed to help people walk through similar trials, and the enemy of Identity Theft would "be trampled down like mud in the streets." We petitioned that because Zachary had warred for so long and it had been so brutal, he would be able to see others delivered in a month, in a week and even in a day! So, this became our prayer. God granted our request, although we wouldn't know that for a season. And over the years God would unfold how He actually granted us so much more.

"Now to Him who is able to [carry out His purpose and] do superabundantly more than all that we dare ask or think [infinitely beyond our greatest prayers, hopes, or dreams], according to His power that is at work within us…" (Ephesians 3:20, AMP).

PAYBACKS ARE HEAVEN

"The LORD *executes righteousness and justice for all who are oppressed."* Psalm 103:6

You've heard it said, "Paybacks are hell." Well, not in God's economy. God doesn't simply "even the score." He rewards in abundance.

It has been over thirteen years since the night Zachary came into our room and shook us awake. And we are still reaping the rewards from our season of darkness. God is still revealing truths to us and showing us the fruit it has produced—and it has been a bountiful harvest. One such fruit is in your hands now.

It has always been our prayer that God would use our testimony to set others free. God began to speak to me about writing Zachary's story in 2012. At the time, it seemed daunting. I was too raw, and I didn't want to re-live it, even on paper. I continued to run from that request for five years, for one reason or another, until the first edition of my book was written and published in 2017, (under the title *Who Do You Say I Am?*).

While in prayer at a Christian conference the year before, in 2016, God showed me three parents crying over their children. He showed me their faces, and I heard their desperate sobs. I didn't only hear them, I felt their cries in my own heart. I remember God asking me, again, if I would write this book. He said, "If it would help set their children free, would you write it even if only for these *three*?" I remember a sob escaping my throat, as I responded, "Yes. I will write it even for *one*." I can honestly say, if it changes just one life, it will have been worth this labor of love.

You see, the battles we wage and win are meant to break ground for those who walk behind us. They can be a portion of the damages we are awarded in God's court. He longs for us to ask this of Him. *"You do not have, because you do not ask"* (James 4:2, ESV). No one is meant to fight a war against the enemy in vain. God delights in granting our request for redemptive spoils of our warfare.

I remember asking this of God for Zachary. I petitioned God that freedom would come to others through Zach's testimony. I asked for Zachary to be anointed to pray true identity over others and that their breakthrough would come quickly.

In the natural realm, we earn authority to speak to issues about which we have great knowledge and experience. This is where we get the term, "He is an authority on the subject." It's similar in the spiritual realm. When we walk through something with the Lord, God *gifts* us with a spiritual authority in that area.

I'm not speaking of an authority to wield *over* people. This authority is not about standing on a platform for money or praise. It's an authority, given by God, to help people. We become a tool in the Lord's hands as we partner with Him to bring deliverance to others in the same areas we have warred and come through a conqueror.

We are not meant to come through our battles as merely survivors. We are meant to come off the battlefield as victors, and to lead others out to victory, as well.

Earlier, I explained that Zachary would get hit the worst when Richard was gone. The enemy would swoop in when we were most vulnerable, like when Richard was grocery shopping for me or was at work. I had asked God, "Why?" His only answer was, "Because it is your demon to battle, too." I thought at the time this was because I had battled fear my whole life, and it seemed to be a generational spirit. In my logic, I figured God was trying to have me face fear, to get it out of me.

It wouldn't be until over four years later that I would realize the truth. I was recounting our testimony to someone, as I had numerous times before and since. As I was sharing what God had said to me, and how I had interpreted it, God interrupted my thoughts in His all too familiar way. He simply said, "When I told you, 'It is your demon to battle, too,' why did you assume I meant I was using this to weed something *bad out* of you? Why wouldn't you know Me (*yada* Me) and understand it was for Me to pour something *good into* you? It was your demon to battle, too, because it was your victory to win, too. It was your authority to walk in, too."

This hit me like a brick to the chest. I had realized by then what God did *in* Zachary and what He was doing *through* him as a result of this battle. I watched God make him a wise, mighty warrior with great authority over identity theft. What I hadn't realized yet was that it was "my demon to battle, too" because God had spoils of war to gift me with, as well. I, too, had earned authority over the same spirit.

This is the same for you! When you go through a trial—even second-hand with someone you love—you can come before God's judicial "bench" and stand on the legal precedent of His "Law of Multiplied Returns and Restoration." What do I mean by this? The places in your life where the enemy has come in to "kill, steal and destroy" *allow* God to do extravagant things on your behalf to balance the scales of His justice.

God is God. He can do whatever He wishes. Obviously, He does not need permission to bless us. So what do I mean by saying that what the enemy does in our lives "allows" God to give us multiplied blessings?

When God places a law into effect, it sets a legal precedent. He binds Himself by that same law and precedent. And from scripture, God seems to have established a law of multiplied returns for our losses. This is found all through scripture. Here are just *some* examples:

> *"The thief comes only in order to steal and kill and destroy. I came that they may have life and have it in **abundance**, (**to the full, till it overflows**)"* (John 10:10, AMP).
>
> *"If the theft is certainly found alive in his hand, whether it is an ox or donkey or sheep, **he shall restore double**"* (Exodus 22:4).

> *"And **he shall restore fourfold** for the lamb, because he did this thing and because he had no pity"* (II Samuel 12:6).
>
> *"Then Zacchaeus stood and said to the Lord, "Look, Lord, I give half my goods to the poor; and if I have taken anything from anyone by false accusation, I **restore it fourfold**"* (Luke 19:8).
>
> *"Yet if he is caught, **he must pay sevenfold**, though it costs him all the wealth of his house"* (Proverbs 6:31, NIV).

Keep in mind, these scriptures are speaking of man stealing from man. How much more so will God require the *enemy* to pay back *His children*? God has determined to restore multiplied blessings for all that is stolen from us: from living life in a fallen world, from man, and from the enemy himself.

When we repent, God even restores the losses we incur through our own sin and mistakes! He remembers it no more and then demands payback from the enemy! This happened with Saul, who later became Paul. Saul was a persecutor and murderer of believers, who repented and became Paul—who was blessed to lead countless to Christ through his messages found in the New Testament. Amazing! Oh, who is like our God?

But it doesn't stop there. God even gives us multiplied blessings for the things and people we willingly surrender for the sake of Jesus and His gospel. And for that, we do not receive a double, quadruple or a sevenfold blessing. We receive a hundredfold reward!

> *"So Jesus answered and said, 'Assuredly, I say to you, there is no one who has left house or brothers or sisters or father or mother or wife or children or lands, for My sake and the gospel's, who shall not receive a hundredfold now in this time—houses and brothers and sisters and mothers and children and lands, with persecutions— and in the age to come, eternal life'"* (Mark 10:29-30).

So you see, in God's justice system, He doesn't simply put an equal weight on the scale of blessing—opposite our trials, thefts and losses. It would seem God tilts the scales in our favor. He *heaps* blessings on. And in multitudes!

Zachary was told he would come out of his trial with an authority, depth and anointing *greater than* the battle he waged and had victory in—and that one day he would have great spiritual authority to set captives free from the same spirit. And since it was my demon to battle, too, I was blessed with the same!

The very fact that God was not coming in and "saving the day" at the beginning of Zach's trial was actually storing up greater blessing, godly authority and anointing in his life. In God's justice system, it is the battle with the lions, bears and the giants of the land that equips us to be kings.

"WHAT'S STOPPING YOU?"

> *"Behold, I give you the authority to trample on serpents and scorpions, and over **all** the power of the enemy, and nothing shall by any means hurt you"* (Luke 10:19).

When I read this verse, I hear God say, "All power over the enemy means…ALL power over the enemy." I have contended for years that this verse and others like it would be my *yada experience*, not simply my head knowledge. Why is the Word sometimes so contrary to our experience? What keeps us from walking in these scriptures and promises?

In January of 2013, while Zachary was in his first year of ministry school, I called my friend Barb on the phone. I presented these questions:

"If these scriptures are true, what is preventing them from becoming a reality in our lives? What keeps them from being our lifestyle? What are we missing or doing wrong?"

Literally a couple of hours later, my friend Carrie called me from California. She began to tell me a dream she had that week. In the dream, she was with Jesus. He asked her the same question over and over again, "If 'this' is true, what stops you from being anointed?"

She didn't know the answer to Jesus' question. She knew within the dream that 'this' pertained to scriptures like I listed above. "*If* these scriptures are true," Jesus was asking her, "what is stopping you from being *anointed* and *walking in them*?" Again, she told Jesus she didn't know. Jesus turned around and called out to someone saying, "Go get me Thomas." In the dream, my friend knew Jesus was asking for "Doubting Thomas" to come speak to her, and then she woke up.

So there it was. There was her answer. There was mine. Doubt. So how do you overcome doubt? How do you believe with all your heart when you, too, have had a traumatic loss or experience? How do you believe God will not only restore, but give you multiplied restoration and an authority in the very area you've battled?

As I shared in earlier chapters, it begins with an intimate friendship with God, as opposed to merely knowing *about* God. It begins with *yada*. We must spend time with Him so we can move past knowing with our minds that God restores, to *yada* the God who restores all things; to move past knowing that God never leaves me nor forsakes me, to *yada* the LORD who is always with me. Our doubt washes away as we behold Him, as we come into His presence and sit at His feet, and as we *yada* each facet of His nature and character.

The enemy will do whatever it takes to keep you from your destiny or to cause you to lay down your gifts and callings. He will try to get you to defer your destiny to another time, place or person. There are times when God calls you to lay something down that He has promised you, but only for a season. It is not meant to be forever.

Never let your God-given dreams die in your heart. Life, loss, attacks, the enemy, our lack of faith, and even our own sin—if repented of—cannot keep us from walking in the destiny of our gifts and callings, if we will but believe.

"For the gifts and the calling of God are irrevocable" (Romans 11:29).

"If we are faithless, He remains faithful; He cannot deny Himself" (2 Timothy 2:13).

He cannot deny all that He is. He cannot cease to be faithful, kind, merciful, generous and extravagant in His love toward us. No matter what we have done or what has been done to us, He cannot stop being all He is—in us, through us and for us.

"I would have despaired had I not believed that I would see the goodness of the LORD in the land of the living. Wait for and confidently expect the LORD; Be strong and let your heart take courage; Yes, wait for and confidently expect the LORD" (Psalm 27:13-14, AMP).

NOW WHAT?

1. Have you suffered losses at the hand of the enemy? Go before the Lord, in prayer, as your Just Judge. Ask God to show you if there is a just cause for the attack (if there is anything you need to repent for, so your record can be expunged).
2. As God reveals things to you, spend time with Him processing through them. Sometimes we have been terribly hurt and

wounded, but have responded in sin. (As I sinned during Zach's dark season by accusing the Lord, judging Him falsely for apparently not intervening, and speaking to Him with dishonor—even when in the quietness of my heart.) When we repent for our sinful responses, we will not only find forgiveness, but healing as well.

3. Once you feel that your record is thoroughly expunged through repentance, ask Jesus to plead your case on your behalf. Talk to the Lord, in faith, about what you would like in court-appointed restitution for your damages.

4. Ask in faith, if desired, for part of your restitution to be an authority to help others who are battling similar trials and spirits. Ask God for your breakthrough to be their breakthrough, and for your victory to allow for a quicker victory for them.

   As an example, I asked for Zachary to be able to counsel and pray for those who have also suffered at the hands of an identity theft spirit. I prayed Zach would do damage to the enemy and that the testimony of his personal breakthrough would pave the way for others to find breakthrough. In God's multiplied justice, what the enemy has been able to do to one, God can turn around and use to rescue and bless many. And since "it was my demon to battle, too," I asked God for my testimony to accomplish the same.

5. In faith, thank God for His law of multiplied restoration, as seen in His Word. Thank Him for what He will do in your life—and in the lives of your physical and spiritual children—as a result of your time before His court.

6. Jesus could be asking you the same question He asked my friend in her dream, "If this is true, what is stopping you from being

anointed?" As He brings His words of truth before you, ask yourself this question: "What is stopping me from believing and walking in these truths?" He is a *good* Father. He is a better parent than me. A better parent than you. His words are truth and life. So what is stopping you? Dare, my friend, to believe!

PRAYER

Dear Father, I come before Your throne as my Just Judge. I thank You for Jesus' blood, shed for me. I ask You to open the books and reveal to me if the enemy has any just cause for what he has sown in my life. Search my heart and see if there be anything in me that would give him legal entrance.

Help me to process through whatever You show me. Give me the faith and courage to do business with what You reveal in Your kindness. Help me to forgive where I need to forgive and to repent where I need to repent. Lord, reveal to me where I have been wronged, but have had sinful responses as a result. Help me to repent for those sinful responses.

Guide me in walking through repentance and healing for my wounded heart. Where there is trauma in my life that has taken up residence in my body, I ask You to wash and cleanse it from me. Heal my heart and memories, and show me where You were in my darkest nights. Reveal to me Your heart for me as I cried in silence. Please begin a work in me to remove any residue of this trauma from my spirit, soul and body.

Lord, thank You for cleansing me and covering my sins under Your blood. Through my repentance and Your blood, I ask for my sins to be expunged from my record. Father, I ask that Jesus would plead my case on my behalf. I ask for Your court-appointed restitution for my damages. Lord, I ask that You would give me an authority to bring victory to others who are battling the same spirit and trials I have. Bring me out a conqueror, so others can come out conquerors after me, because I have blazed a trail for them. I ask You for my breakthrough and that one day, my victory would be another's victory.

I thank You, in faith, for bringing multiplied restoration for my losses. Not because of who I am, but because of who *You are*. I long to *yada* the God of multiplied restoration.

Lord, show me the places of unbelief that stop me from being anointed. I ask for a gift of faith. Lord, I believe. Help my unbelief. In Jesus' name I pray, Amen!

CHAPTER EIGHT

The Hunted Becomes the Hunter

*And what more shall I say? For the time would fail me to tell of Gideon and Barak and Samson and Jephthah, also of **David** and Samuel and the prophets: who through faith subdued kingdoms, worked righteousness, obtained promises, **stopped the mouths of lions**, quenched the violence of fire, escaped the edge of the sword, **out of weakness were made strong**, **became valiant in battle**, turned to flight the armies of the aliens.*

~Paul, Hebrews 11:32-34

Throughout the summer of 2012, Zachary continued getting stronger. After walking through a year of darkness, the first light of dawn came in the night through his dreams. As I shared earlier, Zach had been having recurring nightmares about being attacked by a bear. I chose to take heart that Zachary was showing signs of progress in direct correlation to the battle he was waging with the bear as he slept. Zachary's dreams were indeed becoming less and less vicious, but the fact he was still having them was disconcerting.

Periodically Zachary would awaken and share his dreams, especially if there were significant changes to his nightmares with the bear. One morning as he spoke, my spirit leapt within me. Usually Zachary's bear nightmares ended with the bear injuring him to one degree or another. But on the previous night, it had ended quite differently. Zach had grabbed the bear's head between his hands, looked the bear square in the eyes and said, "I'm *not afraid* of you, anymore!" and snapped the bear's neck. The bear dropped to the ground—dead—never to resurface in his dreams again.

I knew God had given us a sign. I didn't know how or when, but something monumental had shifted in the night, and it would soon make its way into our day.

BECOMING DAVID

In June of 2012, we had given Zachary a leather-bound Bible to commemorate his graduation from high school and his acceptance into ministry school. We wanted it to signify all that Zachary had gone through over the last year, and what we believed would come to pass in the next season. The scripture at the top of this chapter became like a prayer—a prophetic declaration—over Zachary's life. So we engraved it on the cover:

Zachary David Smeltzer
Hebrews 11:32-34

As summer wound down and we approached the day Zachary would be leaving for ministry school, my heart grew increasingly heavy. I tried not to think about it. But Zachary's identical twin, Jacob, was also leaving home to start college, and I would be losing two sons to two different schools. To say my heart was breaking and filled with concern and a sense of loss was an understatement.

On August 29th, after Richard had gone to bed for the night, Zachary and I decided to stay up late and watch a sermon given by Pastor Bill Johnson—the same Bill Johnson who prayed for Zachary less than a year previous—entitled "Supernatural Rest." At the end of the message, Pastor Bill shared that he had heard a sentence as he awoke from his sleep one morning. He felt it was God speaking of Himself. The sentence was, "He watches over the watch of those who watch the Lord." He went on to ponder what God was saying. He realized God was showing him that as he kept his eyes on the Lord, God would watch over his concerns and those he loved.

He said he felt there were some listening who had been tormented in the night for quite some time. He encouraged them to get prayer. He requested those who were praying to declare an end to their dark season. He felt God was saying, "Enough is enough. It ends tonight." Pastor Bill encouraged those praying to declare a shift of seasons, beginning from that point forward.

I couldn't believe how timely this message was. Not only for Zachary, but for me. Zachary would be leaving Idaho for California in a few days to begin a new chapter in his life. And as his mom, I desperately needed to believe "God would watch over my watch, as I kept my eyes on the Lord."

Zachary and I decided to do as the pastor suggested and pray for each other. We had both been tormented for over a year, and we were more than ready to lay down our swords for a much needed rest. Zachary prayed over me and said, "Today marks the day that, as a mom, you will lay down your worry for your sons, in rest and trust that the Lord will take care of them." Zachary added that God would amaze me with the tangible ways He would display this, and I would give God praise as a result.

I then prayed over Zachary that the season of him fiercely battling the enemy was over. I declared he was coming into a new season, where he would be the one causing damage to the enemy—that the hunted would now be the hunter. I prayed for the authority Zachary gained in his last season to be made manifest in his life that coming year. I remember looking into Zachary's eyes and saying, "The enemy will be sorry he ever messed with you, because of what God will do through you as a result of his attacks."

As we headed off to bed, Zachary told me he would be gone hunting when I woke up the next morning, so not to worry. We hugged goodnight, and I went to bed praying God would indeed give me the faith to fully turn my son over to Him from that night on.

I knew it would take a miracle. I was a mother whose son was about to leave the nest for the first time, and he would be 12 hours away. That is difficult under normal circumstances, and our circumstances over the past year had been anything but normal. So I fell asleep that night meditating on the Lord and His goodness, asking God, again, to "watch over my watch," and praying He would protect Zachary the next day as he hunted.

Zachary hunts for food—not for trophies—and with archery season opening the next day, he had planned to rise early to hunt the woods on the other side of the street behind our home. The property he would hunt on belonged to an elderly couple, Roy and Helen. Roy was a fighter pilot in the Korean War, and Zachary had formed a relationship with the couple over the years. Every year, they allowed Zachary to bow hunt the woods on their property. This was a blessing, because Zachary could simply walk out the back side of our property to his hunting ground.

Because it was archery season and private property, Zachary didn't take a sidearm or a knife. There was no need. We live in a safe neighborhood, and there are no dangerous animals in our area.

All through Zachary's dark year, we had reminded him he was a David—almost daily, with the strategy God had given me. On Zachary's way to hunt that morning, he said his mind was pondering the story of David killing the lion. He was marveling over the fact David killed it with his bare hands. He was thinking about how hard that must have been, and the thought entered his mind, "What would I ever do if I came into contact with a lion?" He was not feeling as strong as David at the thought. No worries. He was simply hunting deer, practically in his own backyard.

He set up and waited. After a couple of hours, he spotted a large buck traveling with some does. He nocked an arrow and readied his bow, waiting patiently for the buck to come into the open for a clear shot. It was then that other deer began making a warning noise, indicating they sensed danger. Zach looked around, trying to figure out why. He was pretty sure he had been careful enough to avoid being seen or smelled by the deer, and he was on private property by permission, so he knew there were no other hunters.

Much to his relief, he heard a rustling in the brush behind him, which made him think that maybe the buck hadn't been spooked and was still going to come into the clearing. With his arrow already nocked, he whipped around. But instead of the expected buck, he locked eyes with a mountain lion! The lion was only 14 feet away—crouched low, moving toward him, and ready to pounce.

Instantly, a supernatural peace washed over Zachary. Usually when he goes to shoot, he thinks through the shot and adjusts his bow. This time, there was no time for that. Zachary said he immediately heard God's still small voice saying, "Shoot now." It was a kill or be-killed moment. Without pausing to question the command, Zachary released his arrow. It flew with amazing precision, hitting the lion and sending it fleeing into the trees.

He later shared that in the moment, he had no fear and felt no anxiety—in spite of the very real threat to his life. It wasn't until he was on his way home to get help tracking the lion from Richard and our family friends, Andrew and Wilburn, that he started shaking. God had given Zachary "supernatural rest" in the presence of his enemy, and He had watched over my watch simultaneously.

I remember the emotions I had when I first laid eyes on that lion. I know the enemy meant to take out my son that day, and it is still a sobering thought. But in God's strength, my son took out the *enemy* instead! I think back so many years ago to that 2-year-old little boy who was afraid to go to sleep because of the lion and the bear. How I had prayed for him and beseeched God to make it go away. I think back to the entire year of nightmares Zach had from 2011-2012, when the bear ripped my son apart as he slept—leaving him bloodied on the ground and often missing a limb.

I hadn't understood what good could come from any of it. But all that time, what the enemy meant for evil, God had extravagant plans to turn for good. God was preparing my son to be a mighty warrior.

> *"And we know that all things work together for good to those who love God, to those who are the called according to His purpose"* (Romans 8:28).

When the four men went to look for the lion, they came across its den right there on Roy and Helen's property. The opening was big enough for the men to climb down, and the inside was littered with the bones of the neighborhood pets it had been feeding on. They moved on from there and finally found the animal dead and lying in the brush. Zachary and Richard immediately contacted Fish and Game, who came out and conducted an investigation. The investigation proved Zachary had responded in self-defense, which was important because Zachary did not have a tag to hunt a mountain lion.

When the game warden came out, he comforted Zachary by explaining to him that the fact the lion had made its home in a residential area was very serious. When a wild animal does so, even if relocated, they often do so again. Because of this, the game warden explained, they usually have to put the animal down. He would go on to tell Zachary that this was the first incident of a mountain lion being reported in our neighborhood. They were stunned. They also expressed gratitude that Zachary was the one who first came upon the animal and not Roy or Helen. The story could have ended quite differently.

When I saw the size of the lion's paws and its dagger-like teeth, I started to cry. That thing was stalking my son! The men measured it and found the lion to be 7 feet long exactly, nose to tail. It is interesting to note that the number 7, according to scripture, is the number for completion. And something in the spirit had definitely been completed that day.

I realized it was by the grace of God my son was still alive. God had faithfully watched over my watch as I kept my eyes on the Lord, and while I was "at rest," sleeping. The enemy had tried to take Zachary out one last time, right before he left for ministry school. But instead, God revealed Himself to Zachary as "the LORD who is with me," and "the God who never leaves me nor forsakes me." These names of God that I had taught Zachary through God's divine strategy, Zachary had now come to *yada*.

Our prayers from the night before started coming to pass *in a day*! That is one of the many attributes of God that I love. Though it seems all is lost and your trial has gone on for an eternity, and though it seems your circumstances are impossible and will never change, God is the God of the suddenly. I love to say, "With God, everything can change in one day. That's all it takes. One day."

My son spent over a year being a terrorized teenager. Yet in the span of one day, he had become a man. He spent the year battling a bear, a lion and the Goliath of Identity Theft, and right before my eyes my son had become…David.

EYES TO SEE

People constantly comment on the favor my family has with God. Sometimes it has been met with jealousy. Sometimes it draws prayer requests and deep needs. Do we have some sort of *in* with God others don't possess? No. We are *all* special to the Lord. We can *all* go to God directly, hear His voice and find answers to our prayers. We can *all* walk in God's favor and blessing. If we are His children, we possess this already. I believe much of what others see as favor, I see as a normal day of being His daughter.

We have all witnessed people asking for prayer during an illness or trial. Time and again I have seen God answer these prayers, only for Him to be forgotten and given no credit when He answers. God's miracles are chalked up to the amazing doctor, medicine, book, coincidence or even worse—the person's own intellect and ability. I have been guilty of these *very same things*. It's human nature. It is even found in Scripture, when ten lepers are healed in Luke 17:11-19.

> *"Now it happened as He went to Jerusalem that He passed through the midst of Samaria and Galilee. Then as He entered a certain village, there met Him* **ten men who were lepers**, *who stood afar off. And they lifted up their voices and said, 'Jesus, Master,*

have mercy on us!' So when He saw them, **He said to them, 'Go, show yourselves to the priests.'** *And so it was that* **as they went, they were cleansed**. *And* **one of them**, *when he saw that he was healed*, **returned, and with a loud voice glorified God, and fell down on his face at His feet, giving Him thanks**. *And he was a Samaritan. So Jesus answered and said, 'Were there not ten cleansed? But where are the nine? Were there not any found who returned to give glory to God except this foreigner?' And He said to him, 'Arise, go your way. Your faith has made you well.'"*

Notice Jesus didn't lay hands on these lepers or pray for them directly. He sent them to the priest and they were healed *as they went*—as they obeyed His strange command. It would be so interesting to know the rest of the story, as to who and what received recognition and honor for the healing of the other nine. But only *one had eyes to see* Jesus as Healer—only *one* came back, fell on his face before Jesus and gave Him thanks and praise. The rest somehow missed the fact the miraculous and loving hand of God had just profoundly touched their lives. Or even worse. They noticed, but they just didn't care to have a relationship with their Healer—at least not until their next crisis.

The night before Zachary's brush with death, I had prayed and declared the season of Zachary fiercely battling the enemy *over*. And I had strongly felt God leading me to do so. I declared Zachary no longer "the hunted." Zachary prayed over me that I would be able to rest and trust God to protect my kids and lay my worry down at God's more-than-capable feet.

I could have come away from this traumatic event and thought, "I don't understand, Lord. Last night You gave me faith to pray and believe our long season of attack was over. I put my son in Your hands and trusted You. Yet Zach was almost killed by a mountain lion—not even 12 hours later! He's been tormented for over a year, and now *this*? Why did You allow this? It doesn't seem right."

Instead, I saw an extravagant answer to our prayers. I saw the enemy try to snuff out my son, but my mighty and awesome God took the enemy out instead—by empowering my son's hand. My God prevailed! He did what He promised! His divine strategy had been working all the time, even when I didn't have the eyes to see it. He took my frightened and tormented son and made him a David, just like He had been training me to declare over Zachary the whole year.

I shared this mountain lion testimony with my family and friends when it occurred. It, too, was interpreted by some as special favor with God. But I don't believe that's true.

I think this misconception stems from the fact that it's often hard to recognize God's favor in our own lives. We easily overlook a moment of God's divine intervention. We even misunderstand and see the exact opposite of what God is doing in a situation—as I could have easily done with the near mountain lion attack. We attribute wrongdoing to God in the very area He is giving us an incredible blessing.

How can we be more aware of what God is doing for *us*? First of all, it's important to be intentional to *look* for God's movement in our lives. Then once we recognize it, to come to Him with thanksgiving. But it's equally important, in my opinion, to glorify God with our testimony of it once we notice. This actually brings increase and opens the door to more of the same—in our own lives *and* in the lives of those we share it with.

Think back to the lepers. Only one came back in Luke 17:15-16,

> *"And one of them, when he **saw** that he was healed, **returned**, and **with a loud voice glorified God**, and fell down on his face at His feet, **giving Him thanks**."*

Only one *saw*, returned to give Jesus thanks, and glorified God with a loud voice so others would hear his testimony. Personally, when I experience God in tangible ways like this, I document it and share it in the form of a testimony. Not in every case, but I purpose to try. (In essence, this book is just that.)

When you come to know how kind, powerful and loving God is, you understand that He can't help but be a Good Father. This is the reason I look for Him. I'm His daughter. And I certainly don't want to miss an opportunity to give Him honor and glory with a thankful heart, for all He does for *me*.

Unfortunately, it's easy to miss what God is doing in the midst of our darkest seasons. (Like, sadly, I missed God's kind intentions during ours.) Too often, we only see things through the lens of our own understanding. Or we filter them through the lies our hearts believe about God and ourselves. We can even blame God for wrongdoing in the very places He is actually providing healing, miracles, protection and provision.

Personally, it took me years to have the eyes to see what God was doing and accomplishing through Zach's year of torment. And over a decade later, I'm still having "AHA!" moments and discovering things I didn't realize at the time. I have definitely *not* been perfected in this area. But in this particular situation with the mountain lion, I saw it right away.

Instead of doubting or questioning God for allowing this attempted mountain lion attack to occur, I recognized it for what it was. A miracle! A shift! A breakthrough! It was nothing shy of God's divine, supernatural intervention in our lives. And I wanted to shout it from the rooftops!

I would like to point out here that we sometimes have a warped idea of how life should be. When we go through difficult seasons, we can feel abandoned or forsaken by God. We fall into hopelessness and despair when things don't turn out the way we had hoped or expected. We misread our trials as punishment or God's lack of concern.

We wrestle, in our own strength, to break out of our desperate situations as quickly as possible—and "cheat the butterfly" in the process. If you will recall, while in the thick of it, Zachary told me that he had asked God *not* to remove him from his situation even one day before he would come out completely transformed on the other side.

Zachary somehow understood that his dark, cocoon state was not only producing beauty, but affording him wings to fly. At that point in his process, Zach already had eyes to see the good work that God was producing in him—when I definitely did *not*. He was somehow able—while undergoing intense mental and spiritual torment—to submit to what his Creator was forming in him, while still warring against the enemy's attack.

This astounds me to this day. Zach somehow understood to "let patience have its perfect work."

> *"My brethren, count it all joy when you fall into various trials, knowing that the testing of your faith produces patience. But let patience have its perfect work, that you may be perfect and complete, lacking nothing"* (James 1:2-4).

God promises us beauty for our ashes, (Isaiah 61:3). He promises He will never leave us nor forsake us, (Deuteronomy 31:8). He promises us His peace, (John 14:27). He promises to work all things for our good, (Romans 8:28). He promises us that He will wipe every tear from our eyes when we meet Him in Heaven, (Revelation 21:4). He promises that we will reign with Him for eternity, (2 Timothy 2:12).

But…He has never promised us an easy life in this world. In fact He has promised us quite the opposite.

> *"I have told you these things, so that in Me you may have [perfect] peace. In the world you have tribulation and distress and suffering, but be courageous [be confident, be undaunted, be filled with joy]; I have overcome the world"* (John 16:33, AMP).

Some of our restoration, healing and redemption won't be realized until heaven. But rest assured, nothing we have experienced on earth will be in vain. Nothing will be lost. Absolutely nothing.

I have come to realize that our life—though precious to God—is not our own. We lay it down when we ask God to be Lord of our life. Our life—in reality—is His. Coming to understand and accept this (again, I'm still working on it) changes everything.

The goal is not to have an easy life where everything falls into place and is wrapped up with a pretty bow. Instead, our life is a love offering to the One who gave us life to begin with. Our life is about how well we love Him and others, regardless of what is going on around us. Our life is *His*, for *His* glory.

You already have God's love and favor, my friend. It is not something you must earn. It's something you possess—simply because you are His son, His daughter. May you have "eyes to see" and live to tell the testimonies of God's many marvelous wonders displayed in *your* life!

NOW WHAT?

1. Have you struggled to see God's hand of blessing and favor on your life? Have you sometimes looked at others and thought, "God may do those things for *you*, but He doesn't do that for

me?" At times, has this caused jealousy in your heart? Possibly judgment toward God and others?

Take time to repent before the Lord. Ask Him to help you to release any judgments you may have made—against Him and those whom you see God's hand of favor on.

2. Ask the Lord to help you to see where He has blessed *your* life. Where have you experienced answered prayer, restoration, redemption, healing, provision, etc.?
3. Spend some time before the Lord taking stock of this. Document it by either typing it up on a computer or journaling it on a piece of paper.
4. Spend some time thanking God for each one.
5. Pick one thing He has shown you and share it with a friend or family member, to glorify His name.
6. Pray and ask the Lord to help you to be more aware of His hand on your life. Choose to be "on the lookout" from here on out. When you do "see," respond intentionally. Document it somehow, thank Him with a grateful heart, and glorify His name through your testimony.

PRAYER FOR THE READER

Lord, I pray that You give this precious reader fresh eyes to see their life from heaven's perspective, from Your perspective. I pray You would reveal Your extravagant and miraculous actions on their behalf. And may their breakthrough testimonies—past, present and future—become a strength and encouragement to many. In Jesus' name. Amen.

CHAPTER NINE

Taking Flight

A caterpillar wrapped in darkness endures for promise of flight.

Jacob Smeltzer

THE MOUNTAIN LION incident shifted something dramatically for Zachary. He left a few days later for ministry school in California, and he continued to heal. The wonderful men and women who taught and led this school were completely unaware of what Zachary had been through, or that they were being used by the Lord to dress his battle wounds. I credit a large portion of his complete healing and restoration to what he would learn and experience in those three years until he graduated.

In August of 2013, Richard and I were driving Zachary and our son Andrew back to California for ministry school. It would be Zachary's second year at the school and Andrew's first. (Zachary's twin brother Jacob would attend a few years later, after receiving a dual Bachelor's Degree in both Marketing and Operations Management.)

On the drive between Idaho and California, Zachary's cell phone rang. It was a year, almost to the day, of the lion incident. It was Tim

Christie, an award-winning photojournalist, who was writing an article for American Hunter Magazine. He had contacted Fish and Game asking for situations where hunters came in contact with predatory animals in residential areas. And Fish and Game provided Tim with Zachary's number still on file.

God had been faithful to bring Zachary through a season most people will never have to face. As a family, we so longed to have something tangible to remember this miracle by—something to pass down to future generations. God knows the secret cries of our hearts. He is the God who answers the prayers we don't even think to pray. And here was God, bringing Zachary a chance to tell his story.

> *"Hope deferred makes the heart sick, But when the desire comes, it is a tree of life"* (Proverbs 13:12).

Zachary and the mountain lion became part of the feature article in the December 2013 issue of American Hunter Magazine. The article was entitled: "Meet the Neighbor: A Toothy Menace Coming to Your Backyard." Tim Christie was so taken with Zachary and his story that he came to our house to meet Zachary when he came home on his school break. This article contained pictures of Zachary and the lion. Our family and friends have been able to use the publication to share the rest of this incredible testimony.

Today, Zachary is not the same person. To meet him, you would never guess he ever showed signs of mental distress. There is not even a remnant of his dark season left. The light and joy have returned to his eyes with magnified brightness, and his laughter brings joy to my heart.

I have a friend who is a licensed counselor, who specializes in addiction, drug counseling and drug-induced mental illness. She expressed that she has never seen anyone fully come out of what Zachary experienced. She marveled over the strategy God gave me, saying it's "revolutionary." But how could it not be? It came from the Lord. He is Jehovah Rapha, the God Who Heals. He is the Great Physician. He is the God who uses the simple things to confound the wise. He is the God who gives us beauty for ashes. He is the God who makes *all* things new.

Zachary graduated from ministry school in 2015. While attending, he was blessed to be invited to preach in South Africa and Spain. He was able to go to a state-run drug rehab in Alabama and meet with several of the men, one-on-one. Some even came to the Lord through Zach's visit with them. He counseled a demonically tormented man who had just escaped a cult. The man was set free in under two hours.

What took Zachary a year to battle, God gave Zachary the authority to break off this tormented man in hours! This is exactly what we prayed for and asked of our Just Judge before His courts.

In Zachary's third year of ministry school, he worked with the youth group at Bethel Church in Redding, under their youth pastor. The youth pastor's wife worked with a beautiful girl on the Bethel staff, named Savannah. This youth pastor couple turned out to be the perfect matchmakers. On July 23, 2016, Zachary married Savannah, and we are blessed to have added the first daughter to our family.

After getting married, Zachary worked full time while getting a degree in Business Administration and Management, graduating in 2021. At the time of this Second Edition printing, Zachary and Savannah have two children. Zach works for a successful company as their Marketing Manager and volunteers at his church's weekly youth group meetings. Zach still has a heart for counseling and coaching, and I wouldn't be surprised if he is a pastor one day.

God not only healed and redeemed Zachary through this intense battle, but He forged a deep bond in our family. We all came out closer because of it. Richard and I have a deep trust relationship with our three sons. They feel they can come to us with anything, and that blesses us.

Our sons came out closer as brothers, too. They found a new love and respect for each other. Much of the former competition between brothers came to an end. Now they all share a confidence in God and His power to heal, redeem and restore all things in their lives. Each definitely has his own unique walk with the Lord. Yet each one carries the deep truths God taught us all during this dark season. And they share them with their friends and peers who battle fear and identity theft.

The wisdom Zachary now carries astounds me. It's as if God used his season of darkness to propel him decades ahead. He is a young man who knows his God and knows who he is. It's his heart's cry to help others know the same. I believe he will one day write his own book. For starters, he wrote the Afterword in the back of this book in 2017, when he was 24 years old. I encourage you to read it. It contains some beautiful and insightful lessons he learned through all this.

Zachary is now no longer the hunted, but the hunter. He is no longer a terrorized boy, but a mighty man of valor. Zachary was stripped of his identity by the enemy—by the Principality of Identity Theft. But God gave him a new identity, one he will carry into eternity.

God didn't merely bring Zachary through this battle a survivor—He brought him through a mighty warrior. And this is God's heart for us *all*. God intends to take our trials, our circumstances and our impossible situations, and do something great in us through them. Why? Just because He loves us, and He can't help Himself as a good and faithful Father. If we will only believe!

TWO TICKETS TO PARADISE

On February 6th, 2015, I was on a women's retreat and we were worshipping the Lord. I am not exactly sure what happened to me, but it was significant and like nothing I had ever experienced before. I felt I was given a glimpse of heaven.

What I remember most is that every care of this world seemed ridiculous and ludicrous in Jesus' presence. Every fear, doubt, and worry was completely absent from me—body, soul and spirit. Instead, all my concerns and prayers were a "Yes and Amen" in Christ. This was more than an understanding or even a *yada* knowing. All that resided in every cell of my being was a perfect faith and love—with peace like I thought was not even possible on this earth. I asked the Lord, "What is this? I don't understand what is happening. How can this be?" I heard the Lord respond, "This is my manifest *shalom*."

I had already studied this word for peace in Scripture. I knew what He was saying. Unfortunately, our English language is grossly inadequate to truly translate the Hebrew scriptures. When we translate the word *shalom* in the Bible, it is usually translated "peace." If you study this Hebrew word, however, it means so much more. It means: safety, perfect health, prosperity, peace, rest, welfare, completeness, soundness, tranquility, contentment and friendship with God and man. Quite a mouthful to merely translate as "peace."

So when the Lord answered me that I was experiencing His manifest *shalom*, it made perfect sense. This was what I felt coursing through every fiber of my being. Nothing this world has to offer could compare. Nothing. If this was a taste of heaven, I wished to drink it in. My friend Barb was in the room and said, "I sense it is time to take communion." She was probably about six feet from where I sat, yet her voice seemed to be traveling from a far distance. I knew I needed to open my eyes and take communion, and this—whatever *this* was—would become a memory.

I began to ask the Lord to just take me. I didn't want to "go back." I didn't want this experience with Him to end. I remember telling Him I didn't want to forget it. It wasn't a fear of forgetting the experience. I wanted to take this reality into life with me. I wanted to live from a place where fear and worry were from a distant land. I wanted to live from a place where the things this world and the enemy can throw at you are of no effect. I remember thinking my prayers would be so different if I could stay in this place. But it was only a taste. A taste I long to experience again, but am so thankful for. A taste I contend for, in prayer, to become my earthly reality.

I opened my eyes and took communion, tears escaping my eyes. My friends were completely unaware of my adventure with Jesus. As I took the bread and wine of His covenant, I thought of the following verse. And for the first time, I could *yada* what Paul was saying. And I knew Paul had tasted it, too.

> *"Be anxious for nothing, but in everything by prayer and supplication, with thanksgiving, let your requests be made known to God; and the peace of God, which surpasses all understanding, will guard your hearts and minds through Christ Jesus"* (Philippians 4:6-7).

Almost two years later, I was pondering this experience upon awakening from sleep. And it dawned on me—this was part of God's court-appointed restitution for the hell I had walked through with Zachary. And if this was true, Zachary could ask to experience it, also! Zachary had experienced the trauma of hell and demons. I felt the Lord prompting me that Zachary could ask to experience the joy and peace of heaven, too. I picked up the phone next to the bed and dialed my son.

As I began to explain what I was sensing, Zachary stopped me. "Mom! I went there last night in my dream!" What? I couldn't believe my ears. God makes me laugh. He knew this all along.

Zachary went on to explain that while he was sleeping that night, he spent time with God. He and God had communicated without words. They communicated spirit to Spirit. Zachary would ask a question of God in his heart, and have the immediate answer and understanding from the Lord.

Through this dream experience, God basically dismantled any remnant of the lies the enemy had sown during Zach's trip to hell and subsequent year of assault. God confirmed to Zachary that his salvation was secure and wiped all residue from his soul. Zachary explained that he saw God in human form, but felt that if he moved a fraction, in any direction, he would have seen a different form. He felt he was only allowed to see God in human form because that is all his mind could comprehend. He went on to say, "When I woke up, my body felt like I had been up all night, but my soul feels lighter. Does that make sense, Mom?" Yes, son. It surely does.

Zachary and I had both walked through the valley of the shadow of death, and God allowed us both to experience a taste of heaven. All these years later, God is still giving us vivid displays of His restoration and redemption. I fall in love with the Lord more and more with each passing year. I now see how my 86-year-old friend, Harald Bredesen (now in heaven with his sweet Jesus), could sit across from me at our kitchen table with that perpetual twinkle in his eyes and exclaim, "Kristen! *All* things work together for good for those who love the Lord! *All* things!" They certainly do, Harald. They certainly do! And I, for one, choose to believe.

God continues—to this day—to instruct me and reveal more of His nature, names and character through the events and lessons of that season. I have come to *yada* (know through intimate experience) God in ways that were deep in my soul before, but they have now been branded onto my spirit. I bear the mark of His names. They are a part of me now and cannot be taken from me. He is the Great I AM who continues to astound me with His extravagant love and goodness. When He asks me, "Who do you say I AM?" I answer, "You are my day. You are my Light in the darkness. You are my strength. You are my Healer. You are the air I breathe. You are the song in my heart. You are my LORD and my Savior. You are my Father. You are my best friend. You are the absolute love of my life. You are my everything."

NOW WHAT?

God is saying, REMEMBER!

REMEMBER who I AM!

Remember who you are!

You are my SON!

You are my DAUGHTER!

You are my Kings and my Priests!

Pick back up what you have laid down!

Pick up the authority I died for, so that you might walk in it!

Sure, you have sinned and made mistakes. Yes, you have suffered great losses. But your identity isn't in the sins, mistakes and losses. Your identity is in *Me*! I am a God of Power! I am *always good* and working on your behalf. I am a God of justice! I *will* make the enemy pay! I will bless you extravagantly for all you have suffered. You need only believe!

REMEMBER who I am!

REMEMBER who you are!

OH mighty man of valor!

OH mighty woman of courage and strength!

OH mighty people of purpose, authority and great destiny!

Remember who I AM, and find yourself afresh in Me!"

You are my Gideons, Peters and Davids! You are my Deborahs, Ruths and Esthers! And now I am calling YOU! It is time! It's time to move mountains together! It's time to be intentional and walk in the authority I died to give you! You were born and placed here for such a time as this! Arise and shine, for your light has come!

Rise up into your true identity in Me! Believe me to be *all* that I AM!

All I am *for* you! *All* I am *in* you! And *all* I am *through* you!

REMEMBER and BELIEVE!

PRAYER FOR THE READER

Dear Lord, I pray for the reader of this book. I ask that my family's testimony would be a spirit of prophecy in their life. I ask You to take *all* the trials, hard circumstances, losses, deaths and pain, and bring Your hope, healing and restoration to each one. I ask, Lord, that You would give them a gift of faith for Your "suddenly" to occur in their life. I pray You would manifest Yourself to them as the God of the Impossible, as You have for us. I ask that they would come to *yada* You. Lord, help them to experience the many facets of Your character, in miraculous and tangible ways. Let the truth of who You are forever transform their life, and may they never be the same. I pray they would come to know the truth of who they are in Your presence and see themself through Your eyes.

I thank You, Lord, for all You have done in and through Zachary and me through this experience. Help this dear reader to understand that if You will do amazing miracles in our lives, You will do them in theirs. You have great plans and hope for them, too! They have only to believe. Bless them now, Lord. Show them Your mighty hand. Show Yourself strong on their behalf. I know You will, Lord. You can't help Yourself. It is who You are!

In Jesus' powerful and mighty name, Amen!

AFTERWORD

By Zachary Smeltzer

For my Mom…

I want to thank you, Mom, for stepping out in faith, like you always do, and sharing our story with whoever will listen. You have worked so hard on this book, sacrificed so much, and you do it selflessly. I am so proud of you. But mostly I want to thank you for always being there for me and for being my strength in my darkest season. Thank you for always being there to comfort me, for being patient with me, and for constantly speaking truth into my life. I love you!

For the Reader…

I'm so thankful you read this book and our story. I hope you understand, though, that while I am so thankful for my mom and her role in my healing, this book isn't about my mom. And it isn't about me. It is about who God is. It is ultimately about a loving Father who is true to His Word and character.

I also want you to know I didn't come away from this perfect. I haven't in some way "arrived." God's Word says that in this life we will have troubles and tribulations (John 16:33). And I have encountered new ones since finding victory in the last one. But I *did* come away different. I came away with a lasting trust in God, and a deep knowing that nothing can separate me from His love. I also came away with a deep sense of who I am. I started dreaming with God of a new life, with new possibilities.

Sadly, people often pursue God in tough times and experience breakthrough in their lives, only to then fall away. God rescues them, because it is who He is. But then they quickly go back to their old ways. How do I know? Because this is what I did when I felt I died and went to hell. I called out to Jesus, and He rescued me. But after He did, I went back to my old lifestyle, like a dog returning to its vomit. I then encountered the terrifying circumstances that caused us so much grief.

Why did I do this? Why do *we* tend to do this? Why do we so often seek God in hard times and then abandon Him in good ones? Maybe we simply want the pain to go away. We want to be free of our hardships. So we pursue God only when we need something. But God is not a genie in a bottle. He is a good Father who desires a lasting and personal relationship with us.

When we are in a desperate situation where we have no other options, it is easy to go to God and rely on Him for help. But often, we aren't changed because we don't allow God to transform us in the process: in the waiting for our rescue or healing. Because we aren't pursuing God for who He is, we are pursuing Him for ourselves. God understands that great need draws us to Him. But this must grow beyond our selfish aims, or the process and experience is too easily forgotten.

When the spirit of identity theft attacked me, God could have changed everything instantly, and my fears and torment would have been relieved. But my heart and life wouldn't have been transformed. I wouldn't be who I am today. And I wouldn't know Him the way I do. It may seem hard to believe, but I wouldn't change what I went through for anything. There is nothing in me that would rather be who I was before, or who would be willing to give up the relationship I now have with God.

The truths of who God is, and the truths of who He says I am, are

Afterword

now a part of me. These truths are planted deep in my soul and spirit and are my foundation for life. And now, instead of God simply being an avenue for my salvation and the freedom from my sin and struggles, I desire more of who He is.

Often while waiting for our miracle, we have the opportunity to come to know God in new ways. When impossible situations arise, it can be hard to believe God *will* do something, or *can* do something, on our behalf. But this gives us the opportunity to encounter the God of the impossible. This is what happened with Abraham and Sarah in the Bible.

In Genesis 18:10-13, the Lord appeared to Abraham.

"And He said, 'I will certainly return to you according to the time of life, and behold, Sarah your wife shall have a son.' (Sarah was listening in the tent door which was behind him.) Now Abraham and Sarah were old, well advanced in age; and Sarah had passed the age of childbearing. Therefore Sarah laughed within herself…"

Sarah laughed when she heard she would have the very thing she'd been hoping for her whole life. She laughed. It seemed too big for God, too good to be true. She may have believed it possible in her early years, but God took too long. And now it was an earthly impossibility.

Don't we do that? We look at what is earthly impossible and we believe that means it's past God's ability to intervene. And while we might believe God would do the impossible for our friend, or for someone important, we have a hard time believing God would do the impossible for us.

If you read this book and thought, "This is great for Kristen and her son, but God wouldn't do this for *me*," then your heart could be taking the same posture Sarah's did. You may be laughing at God's promises and miraculous power, at least on your behalf. Sometimes our hearts believe God isn't big enough for *our* situation. We believe our situation is too difficult or hopeless. Or, in truth, our hearts don't believe God is that good or His goodness would extend to us. I certainly was guilty of that.

But He *is* that good. He is a God of the impossible. He is the hope for the hopeless. He is all-powerful and complete love. It is time to start trusting God on a deeper level and to start trusting Him completely.

The truths in this book are for you, no matter where you are in your life, and no matter your knowledge or current relationship with God. Thankfully, with God, it is never too late. If you have lived your whole life without trusting in God, and you are just now beginning to dare to believe in Him or for your miracle, it is not too late. Know that *you* are important to God, and He desires you to go to Him with your needs and questions. No matter how old you are, no matter what you have or haven't done, or how long you have doubted, it is never too late.

In the end with Sarah, God credited *her* with great faith to conceive a child!

> ***By faith*** *Sarah herself also received strength to conceive seed, and she bore a child when she was past the age, because she judged Him faithful who had promised"* (Hebrews 11:11).

God calls this a faith moment for Sarah. But she *didn't* have faith at first. She laughed. Yet at some point, she must have believed, and God rewrote her history. What I see in Sarah's story is that at any point where we begin to believe in God and His promises, God actually rewrites our history! He celebrates our faith, no matter when it enters the picture, and considers it as righteousness.

Afterword

In this moment you have two choices. You can trust in God for your miracle and wait for Him to bring it to pass. Or like Sarah did initially, you can laugh at the possibility of hope in a good and all-powerful God to work on your behalf. And you can continue on in hopelessness.

> 2 Chronicles 16:9 says, *"For the eyes of the LORD run to and fro throughout the whole earth, to show Himself strong on behalf of those whose heart is loyal to Him."*

God is searching to and fro. He is looking at our hearts. He is looking for those who trust in Him. He is looking for people who have even a seed of faith, who are choosing to trust Him against all odds. And God, Himself, even promises to bring increase to our smallest seeds of faith.

When God is searching to and fro, it doesn't mean He is looking to pick a select few. He is searching for *any* and *all* who believe and who are hanging onto hope, no matter their circumstances, to show Himself strong on their behalf.

> King David said, *"I would have lost heart, unless I had believed that I would see the goodness of the LORD in the land of the living"* (Psalm 27:13).

If David hadn't believed he would see God's goodness in his lifetime, he would have given up hope. In the end, you *will* see God's goodness. There *is* light at the end of the tunnel. If you use the tools presented in this book, you will find freedom, because God is who He says He is.

Breakthrough, for me, was not just having my trial stop and the constant battle lifted in the area of identity theft. I learned that breakthrough isn't merely being relieved of something. It also means I've been imparted with something. I've been given something. I am the breakthrough now. Now I carry the victory of my battle inside me, and

I can be the breakthrough for someone else's battle. And this can be your testimony, too. Your breakthrough continues with you becoming light, hope and freedom to those around you.

I encourage you to continue growing in your communion with God. There is nothing more rewarding or fulfilling—that can give your life more purpose—than knowing Him intimately, and thereby knowing the truth of who you are. It is the only place of complete fullness and overwhelming joy. He has a destiny and purpose for your life that can only be found in Him. I encourage you to allow even a simple curiosity to grow into a stronger desire as you pursue Him.

> As Jeremiah 29:13 says, *"And you will seek Me and find Me, when you search for Me with all your heart."*

God is the God of the impossible; the God who moves mountains. There is no limit to His love or His power. And it will take an eternity to know everything about Him.

I pray that you walk in personal freedom. I pray for your breakthrough. I pray for your victory. I pray you not only have a vision for your own life, but a vision for those around you. A vision for something greater. Because your breakthrough is not the end of your story. It is simply the beginning!

I would love to end by speaking a blessing over your life…

I bless you with all God did for me and more. I bless you to stand firm, no matter the trial. I bless you to seek God and find Him in all seasons of your life. I bless you to be transformed by the renewing of your mind. I bless you with the conviction that if God is for you, nothing can stand against you. I bless you with the authority to help bring freedom to those who are suffering as you have and find victory. I bless you to be the miracle for someone else. I bless you to embrace the process. I bless you with eyes to see God's goodness and beauty all the days of your life.

BONUS SECTION

The Ultimate Question

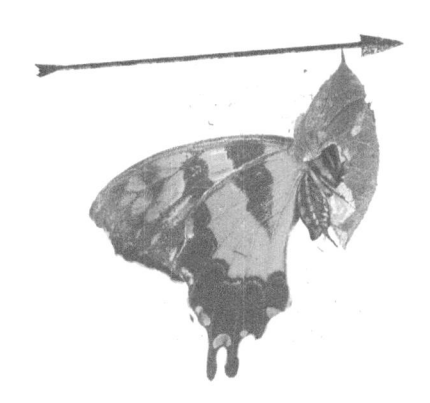

But what about you? Who do you say I am?

Jesus, Matthew 16:15, NIV

THE ULTIMATE QUESTION: A DEVOTIONAL

But what about you? Who do you say I am?
Jesus, Matthew 16:15, NIV

"W*HO DO **YOU** SAY I am?"*

Years ago, the Lord asked me this same question. I had already loved and served Him for decades. I knew all the "right answers." And I would have sworn I believed each one wholeheartedly. Then God lovingly showed me my heart's beliefs.

And it wasn't pretty.

I was standing at the bathroom sink, blow-drying my hair. God dropped one sentence into my mind. He does that from time to time, and it typically sends me on a quest of some sort.

This time was no different. He simply said, *"You think you're a better parent than I am."* It wasn't an accusation. It was more matter-of-fact.

"What?" I replied, bewildered. "I don't think I'm a better parent than You, Lord. In fact, I often feel quite inadequate. Why would You say that?"

Very kindly—but firmly—God showed me my heart. He said, "You would say I am Healer, but your heart says, 'If I was God, I wouldn't have allowed my friend to die of cancer.' You would say I am your Provider, but your heart says, 'If I was God, I would end this season of financial hardship.' You would say I am compassionate, all-loving and all-powerful. But your heart says, 'If I was God, I would change *this*, heal *that*, fix *this*, and not allow *that*.' Your heart says, 'If I was God, I would use my power to do something!'"

My heart was exposed. I hadn't even realized it, but I thought I was a better parent than God, after all. This experience took me on a journey of discovery.

I learned that if my heart believes—even subconsciously—I have more love, compassion or mercy than God, then I have elevated myself above Him and am believing a lie. Any place where I have placed limits on His power, I have humanized Him and reduced Him to what my mind can comprehend. And when I take on a begging posture in prayer, I'm putting my love on a higher plane, by thinking I need to twist God's arm to be as loving and merciful as *me*. Yuck!

When we beg God in prayer, it's evidence we're not believing the truth of who He says that *we* are, either. As His children, we can *ask* of our Heavenly Father, but *begging* is for dogs.

These realizations grieved me deeply, and I asked His forgiveness. My repentance was met with His kindness, as always.

"*Who do you say I am?*" is the most important question of our lives. Why? Because our answer, especially when going through trials and difficult seasons, determines everything. I'm convinced God continually asks this question of each of us. He certainly continues to ask it of me.

Wholeheartedly believing the truth of Him—in all His goodness and glory—is the firm foundation for our lives. Without this foundation, everything that can be shaken will be shaken—including our own identity. Why? Because as people created in His image, we can't know the truth of who *we* are, if we aren't fully convinced of the truth of who *He* is.

While on earth, Jesus walked in the full authority of His identity as the Son of God. Jesus knew who He was because He had a *"yada"* relationship with His Father. The Hebrew word *"yada"* is often simply translated "know" in scripture. But it actually means to "know intimately and experientially."

The Father desires us to *yada* Him, too. This is the sure foundation upon which our identity can stand and weather the storms.

Jesus said of Himself, *"If you had known me, you would have known my Father also. …Whoever has seen me has seen the Father"* (John 14:7 & 9, ESV).

Jesus said, *"I and My Father are one"* (John 10:30, NKJV). There is not an attribute of one that is not the attribute of the other. If you see it in Jesus, then it's truth of the Father. Jesus displayed the Father's true nature and character in how He came, how He spent His time on earth, and in how He died and rose again. Jesus reveals and defines Father God to us.

Anything in our belief system about the Father that contradicts what we see in the life of Jesus is a flat-out lie. These lies all need to be addressed and our minds need to be renewed and transformed.

It's imperative that we wrestle some things out with God in this season. The Bible is full of examples of God's children wrestling out their questions, doubts, and even anger with God. God invites it. And beyond that, at times He even instigates it. One reason is that—in God's mercy and justice—there's always a blessing on the other side of our offenses.

One example is found in John 6:45-68. Jesus said one must eat His flesh and drink His blood to have eternal life. At face value, He appeared to be speaking literally, making a declaration that appeared to contradict the Law. He neither clarified nor explained His meaning. He simply let it sit.

When many of His followers turned away at this point, Jesus asked His disciples, "Do you also want to go away?" The choice was up to them. Each had to wrestle it out in their own hearts. They had to choose to believe the truth of who Jesus says He is—and the absolute Truth of His Words—or walk away.

No manipulation. No begging. No defending. Just a proverbial, "Are you still in? Or are you out?"

Peter answered, *"Lord, to whom shall we go? You have the words of eternal life"* (John 6:67-68, NKJV).

Are you willing to take the same stance Peter did? Will you look at what you don't understand, press past any offenses in your heart toward God, and choose to stay? Can you give Him your "yes," in spite of what you don't comprehend and no matter the cost? Will you determine to take Him at His Word, even when circumstances scream to the contrary?

Sometimes it isn't that easy, right? It can feel daunting to process through our disappointments. The lies we're convinced of, yet may not even be aware of. The places in our hearts where we have given up hope. The places where we're offended with God because He hasn't acted in a way we hoped or expected. How can we begin to wrestle these things out?

Many find conversational prayer or journaling a wonderful tool. What you'll find on the following pages is not meant to tell you what to believe, answer your questions, or wrestle things out for you. Only you, with Holy Spirit, can do that. But it is a tool. A first step.

Who do *you* say He is? Who do *you* know Him to be? Not just in your mind. Not according to your personal theology or church doctrine. But in the depths of your heart? Would your heart reveal you believe you are a better parent than God? A better friend? Would it reveal areas of doubt? Unbelief? Possibly even downright lies?

The following pages are designed to help you discover and process these things. The Lover of your soul is inviting you into a fresh discovery—of His extravagant love, power, kindness and goodness—directed toward *you*.

Be forewarned. This journey is not for the faint of heart. Trust me, I know. Yet it *is* a worthwhile one, I assure you. Let the adventure begin…

LORD, I WANT TO KNOW YOU

FIRST THINGS FIRST

If you haven't read the devotional *The Ultimate Question* (found right before this), please stop and do so. The remainder of this book contains steps to help walk you through where there is a discrepancy between what your heart actually believes of God and what the Word says is true of Him.

Do not be afraid. Have courage to address where what you would maintain to be true of God isn't exactly what you feel to be true in the depths of your heart. The Lord is not angry nor disappointed. He isn't surprised. He knows your heart better than you do.

Instead, He's inviting you to talk it over with Him. He desires you to hash it out with Him, if need be. He's wooing you to truly seek and find Him—and to discover yourself in the process.

PREPARE YOUR HEART

- Set aside uninterrupted time in a quiet place. Have a Bible, pen & paper handy.
- Pray and invite Holy Spirit to speak to you and to guide your time together.
- Read through the list of scripture references containing *God's Names, Nature and Character,* called "*WHO DO YOU SAY I AM?*" (found at the back of this book). Skim through it until

one of God's attributes stands out to you. Is there one you desire Him to be for you in this season? One you struggle to believe?

- Look up the Scripture reference attached to that aspect of His nature in your Bible, possibly in different versions.
- Journal **OR** have a prayerful discussion with God, using the *Conversational Prayer Guide* and the *Journaling Prompts* sections on the following pages.
- It is my hope you will do this as often as you can. This is not meant to be a one-time event, but instead a continuous journey to greater intimacy with the Lord.
- Tip: When we devote time to spend with the Lord, we are often distracted by things to do. Keep a second piece of paper handy. Jot down anything that comes to mind and come back to it later.

CONVERSATIONAL PRAYER GUIDE

WHAT IS CONVERSATIONAL prayer? In a nutshell it's simply talking to God like you would talk to a friend. It's talking and then listening for a response.

That can sound scary to some. But trust me. As you do this more often, you will become more aware of His still small voice. He longs to speak with you, and He desires for you to hear Him. He even promises it (John 10:27 & Jeremiah 33:3).

We are obviously all unique and can go to the Lord in a variety of ways. The following is just one tool to get you started. My desire is to help you walk through any place where you have come to doubt Him or have lost hope in an area of your life.

I pray you will find these tips useful and that you will grow in intimacy with the Lord, as a result.

TALK PERSONALLY

Before you begin, pray and ask Holy Spirit to quiet any spirit not of Him, and for you to only hear His voice of Truth and Love. Imagine Jesus (or the Father) sitting with you as you begin, having a face-to-face chat. (You can choose to do this as a conversational prayer, or you can journal your discussion.)

If you journal it, write down what you are speaking to the Lord and also what you sense Him saying back to you. God will always be kind and loving. If you hear anything else, stop and pray again.

TALK HONESTLY

Be truthful with Him about His attributes that you desire Him to be for you in this season, and also those that stretch your faith. Discuss the places in your heart where you have struggled with a particular aspect of His character and why.

Where does what you've been taught *about* God seem to contradict the truth of His Word? Where does your life experience seem to conflict with what you've believed of Him? Tell Him where you have felt let down, discouraged, abandoned, rejected, afraid and even angry, as it relates to each of His attributes. Be honest. He already knows. *"The Lord will wait that He may be gracious to you,"* (Isaiah 30:18.)

TALK TRANSPARENTLY

What lies have you believed about Him, even unconsciously? The enemy has established "recordings in our head" that will clue you in. For example: We may say we believe God to be all-loving, but if we don't anticipate Him loving *us* in tangible ways, we don't truly believe this. We say God supplies all our needs, but if in financial crisis our first response is panic and to look to our own intellect for a way out, then it reveals a distrust of God in this area.

Our expectation and anticipation of God's interaction in our daily lives reveals the truth of who we consider Him to be. Do some soul searching. Ask the Lord to show you if you believe a lie about Him in the area of a particular attribute.

TALK HUMBLY

The Holy Spirit may reveal areas in your heart where you have become offended with God. Or where, because of pain or disappointment, you no longer hold fast to the truth of His goodness, faithfulness, or love.

Ask Him to show you where He was in the events that brought you to this place. Talk with Him. He desires to bring healing and restoration. Ask God's forgiveness for the areas where you have not believed the truth about who He is. Speak with honor and humility in all this.

I BELIEVE A LIE. NOW WHAT?

If God reveals that you have believed a lie about Him:

- Be specific about the lie you have been made aware of. Name it.
- By faith, ask the Lord's forgiveness for the lie you have believed to be true.
- Make an intentional *choice*—written or spoken—to break an agreement with this lie.

(When we believe a lie in our heart, we are essentially accepting it as "truth"—over God's Truth. This allows that lie to have free reign in our lives. This can be a powerful agreement and almost works like a contract. This needs to be broken, through Jesus' blood.)

- Pray this through.

Sample Prayer:

Lord, I realize I have believed the lie that I have more compassion for those I love than You do. As a result, I have placed my love on a greater plane than Yours. I repent and choose to break an agreement with this lie. Lord, will You forgive me and break the power of this lie in my life? I ask this in the name of Jesus and by His blood. Amen.

- Ask the Lord for the truth that replaces this lie. Wait and listen. Holy Spirit will reveal it to you.
- Pray it through, by making an intentional agreement with the truth He has revealed.

Sample Prayer:

Lord, the truth is that Your love and compassion is all-encompassing. Your love was unto death. No human, not even a mother for her child, could ever love as You love us. I choose, by faith, to come into agreement with the truth that Your perfect love for me and for those I love infinitely surpasses all other love. You, indeed, are Love. Plant this truth deeply in my heart and soul. In Jesus' name, Amen.

- Declare that you choose to believe Him afresh in this area. Ask God to resurrect a faith and assurance in your heart for this truth to be made manifest in your life and in your relationship with Him. *"Lord, I believe; help my unbelief!"* (Mark 9:24).
- Receive God's forgiveness, and let it wash over you.

SAMPLE CLOSING PRAYER

Lord, I ask You to seal the work You have begun today. Jesus, I ask for Your Holy Spirit of Truth to come and renew my heart and mind. Please heal my heart. I ask You to cleanse and bind up my wounds, to renew my hope in You, and to give me a fresh revelation of who You are. Lord, make this beautiful and unique aspect of your nature and character manifest in my life, and "show Yourself strong on my behalf" (2 Chronicles 16:9, NKJV). Lord, I ask that I would come to intimately know (yada) this facet of who You are. In Jesus' name. Amen.

JOURNALING PROMPTS

READ THROUGH THE Scripture list in the back of this book, *WHO DO YOU SAY I AM?: God's Names, Nature and Character*, until one of God's attributes stands out to you. Refer to the previous *Lord, I Want to Know You* and the *Conversational Prayer Guide* sections for further explanation on how to process through these questions. (You can use this same method with the *"Who I Am In Christ"* attributes found in the back, and speak with God about who He says you are, too.)

1. Which of God's names or attributes stands out to me?

2. Is this attribute one I wish God to be for me in this season? One that stretches my faith? One I struggle to believe? Why?

3. Does my heart fully believe this attribute of His character—directed toward *me*? Why? Why not?

4. Has any disappointment, trial or trauma caused me to doubt this? (Tell Him where you have felt let down, discouraged, abandoned, rejected, afraid or even angry, as it relates to this attribute.)

5. Ask Him, "Lord, what do You say about this? Please show me where You were in this circumstance or situation."

6. Ask the Lord, "What lies do I believe about You in this area?" (Be specific about any lie He makes you aware of.)

7. Repent for any lie you have believed of God. By faith, ask His forgiveness.

8. By an act of your will, sever any agreement your heart has held with this lie by the blood of Jesus.

9. Ask the Lord for the truth that replaces this lie you have believed. Wait and listen. Holy Spirit will reveal it to you.

10. Make an intentional commitment to agree with this truth, in place of the former lie. Express to the Lord a conscious choice, by faith, to hope and trust Him in this area.

11. Ask Him to make himself known to you in this way and according to this aspect of His nature.

12. Ask the Lord, "Is there anything else You want to show me or speak about?"

WHO DO *YOU* SAY I AM?

God's Names, Nature and Character

"The name of the Lord is a strong tower; The righteous run to it and are safe."

~Proverbs 18:10

Genesis 14:20a	The Most High who has delivered my enemies into my hand
Genesis 15:1	My mighty shield and exceedingly great reward
Genesis 21:33	The everlasting God
Genesis 22:13-14	Jehovah-Jireh, My Provider
Genesis 28:15	With me wherever I go
Exodus 3:13-14	Jehovah—I AM Who I AM—The Self-Existent One
Exodus 7:5	God who stretches out His hand on my behalf
Exodus 13:3	The God with power to deliver me
Exodus 15:2	EL—The Strong One, My Strength, My Song, My Salvation
Exodus 15:3	The God of war for me
Exodus 15:25b-26	Jehovah-Rapha—The God Who Heals All My Diseases

Exodus 17:15-16	Jehovah-Nissi—The Lord is My Banner
Exodus 18:11	Greater than all the gods
Exodus 22:27	The gracious and compassionate God who hears me
Exodus 31:12-13	Jehovah Mekaddishkem—The Lord Who Sanctifies and sets us apart for Holy use (also in Leviticus 20:7-8)
Leviticus 11:45	Holy
Numbers 7:89	He who speaks from a position of mercy
Numbers 12:6	God who makes Himself known through visions and dreams (also in Acts 2:17)
Numbers 14:18a	Longsuffering and abundant in mercy
Deut. 4:29-31	God is merciful and will be found by me when I seek Him with all my heart
Deuteronomy 7:13-14	The God who blesses and multiplies me
Deuteronomy 7:21-23	The great and awesome God who is in my midst
Deuteronomy 9:4	He who drives out the wicked before me
Deuteronomy 11:14-15	The God who gives me new wine and latter rain
Deuteronomy 31:6	The God who goes before me and never leaves nor forsakes me
Deuteronomy 32:11-12	Holy Spirit who hovers over my life to guide me and bring higher order
Judges 6:11-16	The LORD who is with you
Judges 6:16-24	Jehovah-Shalom—The LORD is Peace, The altar of peace for my fear
1 Samuel 1:3, 17:45	Jehovah-Saboath—The Lord of Hosts, The Lord of Armies

2 Samuel 22:29-31	God whose ways are perfect, who enlightens my darkness, and by whom I can run against a troop
2 Kings 6:17	The God who opens my eyes that I might see the unseen
1 Chronicles 16:25	Great and greatly to be praised
1 Chronicles 29:11	The God of greatness, power, glory, victory, and majesty
2 Chronicles 12:6	Righteous
2 Chronicles 25:9	Able to give me much more than this
Nehemiah 9:16-17	The God ready to forgive, gracious, merciful, slow to anger and abounding in steadfast love
Job 23:13	The God who doesn't change
Job 33:4	The breath that gives me life
Job 33:15-18	The God who opens the ears of men and seals their instruction in dreams and visions
Job 37:2-13	The God who controls nature to accomplish His purposes
Job 42:10, 12	The LORD who restores what the enemy steals from us
Psalm 3:1-8	My shield and help, The God who directs my path when I trust in Him
Psalm 7:10	My defense, defender and shield
Psalm 8	Adonai—My Great Lord
Psalm 9:9-10	The Lord who is a refuge in times of trouble
Psalm 10:16	King forever and ever

Psalm 13:5-6	The God of unfailing love, who deals bountifully with me
Psalm 14:6	The refuge of the poor
Psalm 18:1-3	The Lord my rock, fortress and deliverer
Psalm 18:28	God who enlightens my darkness
Psalm 19:7-9	The Lord whose judgments are righteous
Psalm 20:6	The Lord who saves me with the strength of His right hand
Psalm 20:1-9	The God who answers in the day of trouble and fulfills my purpose
Psalm 23:1-3	Jehovah-Rohi—The Lord Who is My Shepherd; I shall not want
Psalm 23:3	He who restores my soul
Psalm 23:4	God who is with me in the valley of the shadow of death
Psalm 23:5	God who prepares a table for me in the presence of my enemies
Psalm 24:5	The God of my salvation who blesses me
Psalm 24:8	The King of Glory, Strong and Mighty in Battle
Psalm 27:13-14	The God who promises I will see His goodness while on the earth
Psalm 28:8	My saving refuge
Psalm 33:6-9	The God who can create anything from nothing
Psalm 34:8	Good God—taste and see!
Psalm 34:18	The Lord who is near to the broken-hearted

Psalm 36:5	The God whose faithfulness is immeasurable
Psalm 37:28	God of Justice, who does not forsake His saints
Psalm 46	Jehovah-Shammah—The Lord My Companion, God With Us
Psalm 46:10	God in the stillness
Psalm 51:1	He who blots out all my transgressions
Psalm 51:7, 10	The God who washes me whiter than snow
Psalm 56:3-4	The God worthy of my trust
Psalm 56:8	God who puts my tears in a bottle
Psalm 62:6	My rock and salvation, My defense
Psalm 68	Elohim—The All-Powerful One, Creator
Psalm 75:1-7	God is just
Psalm 78:35, 83:18	El Elyon—The God Most High and Kinsman Redeemer
Psalm 89:1-8	God is faithful
Psalm 90:2	El Shaddai—The All-Sufficient One, God from everlasting to everlasting
Psalm 98:1-2	The God in whom is victory!
Psalm 98:9	The unbiased, impartial judge
Psalm 102:25-28	God whose years have no end, perfect and unchanging
Psalm 103:2-3	Forgiver of iniquity and Jehovah Rapha, healer of all my diseases
Psalm 103:12	He who will not remember my sins and is eternally blind to what I've been forgiven of

Psalm 111:4	The Lord who is Gracious and full of compassion
Psalm 113:4-6	God seated high above the heavens
Psalm 119:65-73	God is good
Psalm 121:4	God who neither slumbers nor sleeps
Psalm 139:1-6	God is omniscient
Psalm 139:7-12	El Roi—The God who sees me, Omnipresent
Psalm 139:12	God from whom the darkness cannot hide
Psalm 139:16	The God whose eyes saw my unformed body and ordained my days, writing them in a book before one of them came to be
Psalm 144:1-2	The LORD my Rock who trains my hands for war, my lovingkindness and fortress, high tower, deliverer and shield, He who gives me refuge and subdues people under me
Psalm 145:8	God full of Compassion, Slow to Anger, Great in Mercy
Proverbs 3:19-20	God is wise
Proverbs 3:26	My confidence
Proverbs 8:14	Sound Wisdom, counsel, understanding and strength
Proverbs 8:17	The God who will be found by me if I seek Him
Proverbs 18:24	A friend who sticks closer than a brother
Song of Solomon 2:4	The beloved in the Song of songs
Isaiah 6:1	God who sits on His throne

God's Names, Nature and Character

Isaiah 7:14, 8:8-10	Immanuel—God With Us, "I AM"
Isaiah 9:6	Jehovah-Shalom—The God of Peace, The Counselor, Mighty God, Everlasting Father, Prince of Peace
Isaiah 11:2	The Spirit of wisdom, understanding, counsel and might
Isaiah 25:8	He who wipes away my tears
Isaiah 26:3-4	Yah or Jah—I Am—The One Who is the Self-Existent, The God who keeps me in perfect peace
Isaiah 30:18	The Lord who waits that He may be gracious to me, God of Justice
Isaiah 40:21-26	Powerful Creator who reduces human rulers and princes to nothing
Isaiah 41:4	The First and the Last
Isaiah 41:10	The God who strengthens me when I am afraid and upholds me with His righteous right hand
Isaiah 41:13-16	The God of my help
Isaiah 42:9	God who declares all things new, before they spring forth
Isaiah 43:1	God who calls me by name, who is with me through fire and water
Isaiah 43:13	God before the beginning of days
Isaiah 43:25	He who blots out my transgressions and will not remember my sins
Isaiah 44:6	God, besides Me there is no god, God who is the first and the last
Isaiah 45:6	Adonai Eloheynu, there is none besides Him

Isaiah 46:4	God who carries me in old age
Isaiah 46:10	God who declares the end from the beginning
Isaiah 48:10	God who refines me
Isaiah 48:17	God who teaches me to profit and leads me in the way I should go
Isaiah 51:12-16	God who comforts me
Isaiah 52:6	God who speaks
Isaiah 53:5	The healing I seek
Isaiah 55:9	God who gives me MORE than I can ask or imagine
Isaiah 57:15	High and lofty One who inhabits eternity
Isaiah 58:9a	God who will answer me
Jeremiah 3:12	God who is merciful
Jeremiah 9:24	God who delights in lovingkindness, judgment and righteousness and gives rest for my soul
Jeremiah 23:5-6	Jehovah-Tsidkenu—The Lord my Righteousness
Jeremiah 29:11	The God who gives me a future and a hope
Jeremiah 29:12-14	The God who will be found by me and bring me out of captivity
Jeremiah 32:17	Sovereign Lord—God is omnipotent
Jeremiah 32:27	The God of all flesh, nothing is too hard for Him
Jeremiah 33:6	God who heals me and gives me peace
Lamentations 3:22-27	God whose mercies are new every morning, my hope is found in Him

Ezekiel 24:27b	God who makes me a sign to the unbeliever
Daniel 2:21	The All-Knowing God who controls times and seasons, raises up and removes rulers
Hosea 2:14	God who comforts me in the wilderness
Joel 2:25-27	The God who restores the years the locusts have eaten
Micah 7:8-10	The God who pleads my case and executes justice for me
Zephaniah 3:17	The God who rejoices over me with singing
Malachi 3:6	YHWH—I AM—The God who does not change—when we are faithless, He is faithful

New Testament

Matthew 1:23	Emmanuel, God with us
Matthew 11:4-6	The God in whom the blind see, the lame walk, the lepers are cleansed, the deaf hear, the dead are raised, and the poor have the Gospel preached to them
Matthew 11:19	The friend of sinners
Matthew 16:15	The Christ, Son of the living God
Matthew 16:19	The God who gives me keys of authority
Matthew 23:9	My Father
Matthew 28:20	Always with me and Who keeps me wherever I go
Mark 10:29-30	The God who restores a hundredfold—both now and in the age to come—for all we give up for Jesus
Luke 8:40-56	God who raises the dead

Luke 22:31-32	The God who prays for us that our faith will not fail
John 1:1	The Word
John 1:9	The true light
John 1:14	Full of grace and truth
John 1:29	The Lamb of God
John 1:34	Jesus, the Son of God
John 1:41	Messiah
John 2:7-9	God who turns water into wine
John 3:16	God's only Son, Jesus
John 4:14	The living water
John 4:24	Spirit, worshipped in spirit and in truth
John 6:35	The bread of life
John 8:12, 9:5	The Light of the World
John 8:31-32	Absolute Truth
John 10:9, 14:6	The Door by which I am saved
John 10:10	God who gives me abundant life
John 10:14	The Good Shepherd
John 11:25	The resurrection and the life
John 12:46	The Light who keeps me from darkness
John 14:2-3	The God who prepares a mansion for me in heaven
John 14:6	The way, The Truth, and The Life
John 14:12-18	The God who promises that, if I believe, I will do the works He did and have whatever I ask in His name, The God who will not leave me an orphan
John 14:27	YHWH-Shalom—The Lord is Peace

John 16:13	God who shows me things to come and guides me in all truth
Acts 2:28	The God who makes me full of joy in His presence
Acts 10:42	Judge of the living and the dead
Romans 4:17	The God who gives life to the dead and calls things that are not as though they are
Romans 5:8	The God who loved and died for me while I was a sinner
Romans 8:15-17	God is my Father
Romans 8:27	The God who intercedes for me
Romans 8:28-30	The God who makes ALL things work together for my good
Romans 8:35, 37-39	God is Love, and nothing can separate me from His love
Romans 11:17-24	God is kind
Romans 11:33	God is infinite
Romans 12:15	God who weeps with me when I weep
Romans 16:20a	The God of peace who will crush satan under my feet
1 Corinthians 2:10	The giver of all revelation
1 Corinthians 5:7	My Passover, sacrificed for me
1 Corinthians 10:4	My Rock
1 Corinthians 10:13	Faithful God who will not allow me any temptation that is too strong to overcome
1 Corinthians 15:55,57	The conqueror of death, hell, and the grave
2 Corinthians 1:3-4	God my comforter

2 Corinthians 3:17	The Spirit, abundant in mercy, in whom there is liberty
Ephesians 1:5-8	God is a God of grace
Ephesians 1:17-19	The God who enlightens the eyes of my understanding to see His hope
Ephesians 2:14	My peace
Ephesians 3:20	The God of immeasurably MORE than I can ask or imagine
Philippians 4:13	God who strengthens me
1 Timothy 1:17, 6:15	God who alone is sovereign
2 Timothy 2:13	The God who is faithful when I am faithless
Hebrews 2:18	He who is able to aid me when tempted because He Himself was tempted
Hebrews 4:14-16	My Great High Priest who intercedes for me
Hebrews 5:6-10	Author of eternal salvation for all who obey Him
Hebrews 10:10	He who sanctifies me
Hebrews 10:12-14	The Sacrifice for my sins forever
Hebrews 10:23	The God who is faithful to fulfill His promises
Hebrews 11:6	My rewarder when I diligently seek Him
Hebrews 13:8	The same yesterday, today and forever
Hebrews 13:20	The God of peace
James 1:5	The God who gives me wisdom
James 1:17	The Giver of perfect gifts who is good all the time
1 Peter 1:14-16	Holy

God's Names, Nature and Character

1 John 1:5	The light—in Him there is no darkness
1 John 1:7	The Blood that cleanses me from sin
1 John 1:9	God who is faithful and just, and who cleanses me from unrighteousness
1 John 4:7-10	God is Love
1 John 5:7	Father, Son, and Holy Spirit
Revelation 1:8	He who was, is, and is to come
Revelation 1:18	He who lives forevermore
Revelation 2:7	The tree of life
Revelation 1:18	The God who has power over death
Revelation 4:8-11	God is holy
Revelation 5:5	The Lion of the tribe of Judah
Revelation 5:12	The Lamb that was slain
Revelation 7:17	The Lamb on the throne, who wipes away every tear from my eye
Revelation 19:6	The Lord God Omnipotent, who reigns
Revelation 19:11	Ever Faithful and True
Revelation 19:13	The Word of God
Revelation 19:14	Leader of the armies of heaven
Revelation 19:16	The King of Kings and Lord of Lords
Revelation 21:5	The God who makes all things new
Revelation 22:12-13	El Olam—The Alpha and the Omega
Revelation 22:16	The Bright and Morning Star

WHO DO *YOU* SAY I AM?

Who I Am in Christ

Deuteronomy 7:6	Holy to the Lord, Chosen, A people for God's Treasured Possession
Deuteronomy 28:1-14	Blessed, the head and not the tail
Psalm 17:8	The apple of His eye
Isaiah 43:12	His witness
Ezekiel 24:27b	A sign to the unbeliever
Matthew 5:13-14	The salt of the earth and the light of the world
Luke 10:18-20	Given all authority to overcome the power of the enemy, and nothing can by any means hurt me
John 1:12; 1 John 3:1-2	A child of God, I shall be like Him when Christ returns
John 5:24	One who has everlasting life, who will not be condemned
John 8:31-33	Set free
John 14:12-14	I will do greater works than Jesus if I believe in Him; I can ask anything in His name and He will do it
John 15:1-5	I am a branch attached to the true vine
John 15:14	A friend of God
John 15:16	Chosen and appointed to bear His fruit

Romans 1:7	Beloved of God
Romans 5:1	Justified through faith—completely forgiven and made righteous
Romans 6:1-6	Dead to the power of sin's rule in my life
Romans 6:18	Set free from sin and a slave of righteousness
Romans 6:22	Free from sin, enslaved to God alone (not man or the enemy)
Romans 8:1-2	*Free forever* from condemnation and the law of sin and death
Romans 8:14-15	A son/daughter of God (also in Galatians 3:26, Ephesians 1:5, 2 Corinthians 6:18)
Romans 8:17	Child of God, and a joint heir with Christ
Romans 8:28	All things work together for my good because I love Him
Romans 8:37	More than a conqueror
1 Corinthians 1:8	Brought near through the blood of Jesus
1 Corinthians 2:12, 16	Freely given things by God and given the mind of Christ
1 Corinthians 3:16, 6:19	The temple of God, the dwelling place of God
1 Corinthians 6:17	One spirit with Him
1 Corinthians 12:27	A member of Christ's body (also in Ephesians 5:30)
2 Corinthians 1:21	Established, anointed and sealed by God in Christ (also in Ephesians 1:13-14)
2 Corinthians 2:14	Triumphant in Christ
2 Corinthians 3:18	Being changed into His image

2 Corinthians 5:17	I am a new creation, all things are new
2 Corinthians 5:18-19	Reconciled to God and given a ministry of reconciliation
2 Corinthians 5:20	An ambassador for Christ
2 Corinthians 5:21	The righteousness of God
Galatians 2:20	Crucified with Christ
Galatians 4:6-7	An heir with God and a son/daughter of God, no longer a slave
Ephesians 1:1	A saint (also in 1 Corinthians 1:2, Philippians 1:1, Colossians 1:2, Romans 1:7)
Ephesians 1:4	Chosen, holy and blameless
Ephesians 1:7	Forgiven and my sins are washed in Jesus' blood (also in Colossians 1:12, Hebrews 9:14, 1 John 1:9, 1 John 2:12)
Ephesians 1:11	One who has obtained an inheritance
Ephesians 1:13	Sealed with the Holy Spirit of Promise
Ephesians 2:5	Redeemed, forgiven, alive with Christ, and a recipient of His lavish grace
Ephesians 2:10	God's workmanship, created in Christ to do good works
Ephesians 2:19	A saint and member of the household of God, (I have "refrigerator privileges")
Philippians 2:5	One who has the mind of Christ
Philippians 3:20	A fellow citizen of heaven, seated in heavenly places right now (also in Ephesians 2:6)
Colossians 1:13	Delivered from the power of darkness and now a part of God's Kingdom

Colossians 2:7, 10	Firmly rooted in Christ and complete in Christ
Colossians 2:12	Raised up with Christ and seated in heavenly places (also in Ephesians 2:6)
Colossians 3:3	Hidden with Christ in God
Colossians 3:12	Elect of God, chosen and dearly loved (also in 1 Thessalonians 1:4)
1 Thessalonians 5:5	A son/daughter of light and the day—not darkness
2 Timothy 1:7	Given power, love and a sound mind
2 Timothy 1:9	Called of God with a Holy calling
2 Timothy 2:11-12a	I will live with Him and reign with Him, if I endure till the end in Him
Hebrews 3:1, 14	A holy partaker of the heavenly calling
Hebrews 4:16	Given the right to come boldly before the throne of God's mercy and grace
1 Peter 1:16	Holy and blameless
1 Peter 1:18-19	Redeemed from the curse of the law
1 Peter 1:23	Born of incorruptible seed
1 Peter 2:5	A living stone, a spiritual house, a royal priesthood
1 Peter 2:9-10	A chosen generation, a royal priesthood, a holy nation, God's own possession
1 Peter 2:24	Healed by Jesus' stripes
1 Peter 5:8	An adversary of the devil
2 Peter 1:4	Given exceedingly great and precious promises by God, A partaker in His divine nature.

1 John 5:18	Born with God, The evil one—the devil—cannot touch me
Revelation 1:5b-6	A king and priest
Revelation 21:7	Victorious

ABOUT THE AUTHOR

Kristen Smeltzer is "an ordinary girl with an extravagant God" who has walked with the Lord for over 45 years. She holds a B.A. from Spring Arbor University in Spring Arbor, Michigan. While single, Kristen served on short-term missions with YWAM and also once served as a youth pastor.

Kristen met and married her husband Richard in 1990. Before children, she worked as an elementary school teacher. While raising her three sons, Kristen had 3,000 women under her in a successful direct sales company and was chosen to train the company's top 50 leaders at their yearly convention.

Today, Kristen is an author and speaker who continuously chooses to step out of her comfort zone and jump headlong into unknown territories—to bring hope to the hopeless and God-given identity to His people. Her message will open eyes to the true nature of God and inspire hearers to engage afresh with the Lover of their souls.

Kristen and Richard have three grown sons, one "daughter-in-love," and two beautiful grandchildren. They live near Coeur d'Alene, Idaho.

For more information about Kristen Smeltzer or to contact her for speaking engagements, go to:

www.KristenSmeltzer.com

Made in United States
Cleveland, OH
02 August 2025